Best
BBQ
Recipes

A collection of more than 200 taste-tempting recipes!

Compiled by
Mildred Fischer

GOLDEN WEST
COOKBOOKS

Acknowledgements
Author and publisher gratefully express their thanks to: The American Lamb Council, American National Cattlewomen, Inc., Barbecue Industry Association, Best Foods, Chronicle Features, Desert Mesquite of Arizona, Inc., Goya Foods, Inc., Heublein/Grocery Products Group, Hickory Specialties, Hawaii Ginger Industry Association, Kikkoman International, Inc., The Kingsford Company, Lea & Perrins, Inc., Lucky Stores, Inc., Memphis in May International Festival Barbecue Contest, National Livestock and Meat Board, National Pork Producers Council, North Carolina Pork Producers Association, Old Tucson Corporation, PelFreez Rabbit Meat, Inc., Reynolds Aluminum, Simon & Schuster, and Weber-Stephen Products Co. for their cooperation in the production of *Best Barbecue Recipes*.

Printed in the United States of America
2012 Printing

ISBN13: 978-1-58581-024-6
ISBN10: 1-58581-024-X

Information in this book is deemed to be authentic and accurate by authors and publisher. However, they disclaim any liability incurred in connection with the use of information appearing in this book.

Golden West Cookbooks
(a division of American Traveler Press)
5738 North Central Avenue
Phoenix, AZ 85012-1316
800-521-9221

For free sample recipes from every Golden West cookbook, visit:
www.GoldenWestCookbooks.com

CONTENTS

Beef 57

Chicken 73

Pork 85

Side Dishes **155**

Meet the Author . . . .

Introduction

Introduction

The word "barbecue" has a provocative history. Research suggests it was a word in Taino, the language of aborigines (now extinct) who populated the Greater Antilles in the New World. Whether it is derived also from the Spanish word "barbacoa" (a wooden grid on which meat is roasted) or from a French phrase "barbe a queue" (from beard to tail) is open to conjecture.

"Barbecue" identified a stick platform or wooden framework supported by posts. The platform served a dual purpose. By day, it was used for drying meat. At night, it became a sleeping area. It has served, too, as a scaffold large enough for smoking fish and fresh meats. Many cultures embraced the framework to roast the whole carcass of sheep, hogs or oxen. In earlier times, political campaigns in the United States were highlighted by barbecues for a multitude of voters.

So the word has entered our language in the guise of a noun (Let's do barbecue), a verb (Let's barbecue) and an adjective (barbecued beef). The word itself conjures visions of sizzling meat on a grill, smoky aromas, and tantalizing taste treats.

Tastes for barbecue sauces vary throughout the country, but regional preferences appear to fall into the following categories: Southern states—hot and spicy; Midwestern— ketchup-based; South-western—heavy, hickory-smoke flavored; North and Northwest—sweet, mildly seasoned.

Barbecuing and charcoal grilling are techniques often confused. Barbecuing refers to the method of placing meat over live coals at a sustained temperature of about 200 to 220 degrees. It's a prolonged type of cooking, suitable for "open" or "closed" pit operations. In "open pit" barbequing, a hole is dug in the ground, slow-burning wood is added, bundles of meat are placed on the embers, a sheet of metal covers the bundles, followed by layers of clean earth and burlap.

"Closed pit" barbecuing refers to a closed cooking container which encompasses the meat and the smoldering wood. Charcoal grilling, on the other hand, identifies placing the meat on a grill directly over the coals of a very hot fire. Certain foods lend themselves well to barbecuing—ribs and large cuts of meat— while grilling is handier for hamburgers, steaks and fish fillets.

Preparation of the meat for barbecue has its distinct adherents. Texas barbecue is a process involving dry rubbing and mopping. The "dry rub" is a mixture of salt, pepper and whatever herbs and spices are desired. The mix is literally hand rubbed thoroughly over the entire surface of the meat. "Mopping" refers to dish mops which are used to baste the meats with specific sauces during cooking. The mop insures that the smoky flavor is captured during the basting. As for the sauce, it's sure to contain spices but no sugar or tomatoes.

The choice of meat for barbecue invites controversy. Residents in some states are partial to particular types of meat. In Kansas and Texas, it's beef. In Tennessee and North Carolina, it's pork. Within North Carolina, another controversy rages— which sauce? The eastern part of the state favors a vinegar and salt combination. In the west, vinegar is ignored and a ketchup with brown sugar sauce is applauded.

Of all the meats available, ribs are especially well-suited to barbecue, and run the gamut from spareribs, St. Louis-style ribs, back ribs, baby-back, country-style ribs, short ribs, and lamb and veal ribs. The word "spareribs" refers exclusively to pork cut from the pork belly or side. These have longer bones with less meat than back ribs. St. Louis-style ribs are spareribs with the cartilage removed. Back ribs, cut from the blade section of a pork loin, are the widest and more tender than spareribs. Baby-back ribs are smaller than back ribs. Country-style ribs are the meatiest of ribs, more like a small pork chop than a rib. Short ribs which have been cut from the rib are likely to be more tender than those cut from the plate section. As for lamb and veal, such ribs generally are cut from the breast.

But, no matter how barbecue is cooked or sauced, and no matter what type of meat or fish is barbequing, barbecue aficionados agree that the accompaniments are almost as important as the meat. Cole slaw, potato salad, baked beans, hush puppies, corn bread, white bread, potato chips, rice, dill pickles—try them all.

Let's do barbecue!

Selecting a Grill

Selection of a barbecue grill depends on a number of factors. To begin with, overnight campers will be looking for a grill that is lightweight and portable, while backyard chefs may prefer kettles, square covered cookers or water smokers.

Depending on the number of people to be served, an hibachi or tabletop grill is ideal for two, while a brazier, kettle, covered cooker or cooking wagon would be needed to serve a crowd.

The type of foods to be cooked is another determinant in choosing a grill. For the hamburger, hot dogs and grilled steak crowd, almost any type of grill is adequate. However, roasts, whole chickens and game birds are better barbecued on a rotisserie.

Storage space is another consideration. When not in use, grills should be kept covered in a dry storage area away from weather.

Grills themselves come in a multitude of designs. Simplest is the Tabletop Grill, easy to clean, in a variety of sizes for camping or picnics. Fireplace Grills can be folded flat for easy storage and are compact enough for use in a fireplace. The Hibachi, an Asiatic-inspired cast-iron model, is ideal for small-scale barbecuing on patios and porches as well as at campsites.

Most common are the Brazier Grills, simple in design with their shallow, round grills set on three or four legs with a grid over the coals. Some such grills have escalated design-wise to include half-hoods, covers, electric or battery-operated rotisseries. Kettle Grills (which resemble Dutch ovens) are large, round barbecue cookers with domed covers, useful for conventional charcoal or for dry-heat smoking. Electric and gas grills work year round and require no charcoal. Another reason for their popularity is their heat control.

To round out this compendium of grills, consider the Water Smoker, a dome-type grill which employs a pan for liquid. As foods cook slowly on the grill, meat juices drip into the pan and the resultant vapor combined with smoke permeates the meat.

So, the selection lends itself to a variety of tastes and pocketbooks!

Selecting a Grill

Recipe:_____

From:_____

Ingredients:

_____ _____

_____ _____

_____ _____

_____ _____

_____ _____

Directions:_____

_____

_____

_____

_____

Recipe:_____

From:_____

Ingredients:

_____ _____

_____ _____

_____ _____

_____ _____

_____ _____

Directions:_____

_____

_____

_____

_____

Sauces, Rubs, Mops and Marinades

Sauces, Rubs, Mops and Marinades

Laveen Zesty Barbecue Sauce

Betty Accomazzo – Laveen, Arizona

1 medium **Onion**, chopped
2 tbsp. **Butter**
2 tbsp. **Vinegar**
2 tbsp. **Brown Sugar**
4 tbsp. **Lemon Juice**
1 cup **Ketchup**

3 tbsp. **Worcestershire Sauce**
1/2 tbsp. **Mustard**
1/2 cup **Water**
1/2 cup chopped **Parsley**
Salt and **Cayenne Pepper** to taste

Brown onion in butter. Add remaining ingredients and simmer for 30 minutes. Makes enough sauce for four pounds of meat.

Easy-Made Barbecue Sauce

National Pork Producers Council

1 cup **Ketchup**
1 cup **Water**
1/2 cup finely chopped **Onion**
1/4 cup **Cider Vinegar**
2 tbsp. **Light Brown Sugar**
1 tsp. **Paprika**
3/4 tsp. **Liquid Smoke** (or to taste)
1/4 tsp. **Celery Seed**
6 to 8 drops **Hot Pepper Sauce** (or to taste)

Combine ingredients in saucepan. Bring to simmering stage. Simmer about 15 minutes to blend flavors and thicken slightly. Makes two cups sauce.

Tip: Prepared mustard is a mixture which is different from dry mustard or ground mustard. It combines whole, cracked or ground mustard seed with vinegar, wine, water, beer or grape juice. At times there are other ingredients as well. In Britain it is known as "made mustard." In the USA, it is generally made with white seed, sugar, vinegar, and tumeric (to make it yellow).

Sarah's Special Sauce for Pork

Dr. Sarah E. Leak – Charlotte, N.C.

1 tsp. **Brown Sugar**
1 tbsp. **Paprika**
1 tsp. **Hickory Smoked Salt**
1 tsp. **Dry Mustard**
1/2 tsp. **Chili Powder**
1/8 tsp. **Cayenne Pepper**
2 tbsp. **Worcestershire Sauce**
1/4 cup **Vinegar**

1 cup **Tomato Sauce**
1/4 cup **Ketchup**
1/2 cup **Water**
Dash **Red Pepper**
Dash **Tabasco® Pepper Sauce**
1 **Bay Leaf**
2 **Cloves**
1/8 tsp. **Lemon Juice**

Combine all ingredients and simmer for 15 minutes. Remove bay leaf and cloves before using to baste pork.

Polynesian Teriyaki Sauce

Kikkoman® International, Inc.

1/2 cup **Kikkoman® Teriyaki Sauce**
1/3 cup **Apricot-Pineapple Preserves**
1/2 tsp. **McCormick® or Schilling® Ginger**
1/8 tsp. **McCormick® or Schilling® Garlic Powder**
1 tbsp. **Cornstarch**
1/4 cup **Water**

Combine first four ingredients in saucepan and bring to a boil slowly. While sauce is cooking, combine cornstarch and water and add to sauce. Cook until sauce thickens. Makes one cup sauce.

Charcoal Barbecue Sauce

Marjorie Shepherd – Magnolia, Arkansas

1/3 cup **Worcestershire Sauce**
2 tbsp. **Tabasco® Pepper Sauce**
2 tbsp. **Red Hot Sauce**
4 tbsp. **Brown Sugar**
1/4 cup **Lemon Juice**
1/4 lb. **Margarine**
1 tbsp. **Mustard**
1 bottle (32 oz.) **Ketchup**

1 **Onion**, grated
1 tsp. **Barbecue Seasoning**
2 cloves **Garlic**, grated, with juice
1 tsp. **Barbecue Spice**
1 cup **Hickory Smoke Barbecue Sauce**
Pinch of **Garlic Powder**

Combine all ingredients in a heavy boiler and mix thoroughly. Cook for about 3/4 hour, stirring occasionally. Makes about two quarts.

Honey Spiced BBQ Sauce

Steven R. Sutter – Bluffton, Ohio

1 1/4 cups **Ketchup**
2/3 cup **Salad Oil**
3/4 cup **Vinegar** or **Red Wine**
5 tbsp. **Worcestershire**
1 cup **Honey**

2 tbsp. **Dry Mustard**
3 tsp. fresh grated **Ginger**
1 **Lemon**, sliced thin
3 tbsp. **Butter**

Combine all ingredients in a saucepan and heat to blend together. Makes enough sauce for four pounds of hamburger meat.

Barbecue Sauce

*Walter Jetton's LBJ Barbecue Cook Book
(Courtesy Simon & Schuster)*

1 cup **Ketchup**	3 **Bay Leaves**
1/2 cup **Cider Vinegar**	1 clove **Garlic**
1 tsp. **Sugar**	2 tbsp. chopped **Onion**
1 tsp. **Chili Powder**	4 tbsp. **Butter**
1/8 tsp. **Salt**	4 tbsp. **Worcestershire Sauce**
1 1/2 cups **Water**	1 tsp. **Paprika**
3 stalks **Celery**, chopped	Dash of **Black Pepper**

Combine all ingredients and bring to a boil. Simmer about 15 minutes. Remove from heat and strain. This is a table sauce to be served with beef, chicken, or pork. Do not cook things in it. Makes about 2 1/2 cups sauce.

Classic Barbecue Sauce

Courtesy Lucky Stores

1/2 cup **Vegetable Oil**	2 tbsp. **Brown Sugar**
1/4 cup **Vinegar**	1 tbsp. **Chili Powder**
1/4 cup **Worcestershire Sauce**	1 tsp. **Sugar**
1 can (8oz.) **Tomato Sauce**	1/2 tsp. **Seasoned Salt**
2 1/2 tbsp. minced **Onion**	

Combine all ingredients. Let stand five minutes. Stir before using to brush on chicken or turkey parts. Serve with remaining sauce. Makes two cups.

Carolina Style Barbecue Sauces

North Carolina Pork Producers Association

Different areas of North Carolina indicate a distinct preference for certain types of sauces. The following recipes reflect these preferences.

Basic Eastern-Hot Vinegar Barbecue Sauce

2 quarts **Cider Vinegar**
1 1/4 to 1 1/2 oz. crushed **Red Pepper**

Salt and **Black Pepper** to taste

Mix all ingredients well. After basting pig, pour remaining sauce in small jars to serve with cooked pig. Yield: 2 quarts

Piedmont-Lexington-Style Sauce

1 1/2 cups **Distilled White** or **Cider Vinegar**
10 tbsp. **Ketchup**
Salt to taste, if desired
Fresh **Ground Pepper** to taste
1/2 tsp. **Cayenne Pepper**
Pinch of crushed **Hot Red Pepper Flakes**
1 tbsp. **Sugar**
1/2 cup **Water**

Combine all ingredients in a small saucepan and bring to a simmer. Cook, stirring, until the sugar dissolves. Remove from the heat and let stand until cool. Spoon a small amoung of the sauce over barbecued meats. Yield: 3 cups.

Western-Ketchup-Based Barbecue Sauce

1 cup **Ketchup**
1 cup **Brown Sugar**
1/2 cup **Lemon Juice**
1/2 stick **Butter**

1/4 cup minced **Onion**
1 tsp. liquid **Hot Pepper Sauce**
1 tsp. **Worcestershire Sauce**

Place all ingredients in heavy saucepan and bring to a boil. Reduce heat and simmer for 30 minutes. Yield: 3 cups

Kathy's Bar-B-Que Sauce

Kathy Curtis – Houston, Texas

3 tbsp. **Margarine**
1/2 cup diced **Onions**
1 cup **Tomato Puree**
3 tbsp. **Worcestershire Sauce**
1 1/3 cups **Ketchup**
3 tbsp. **A.1.® Steak Sauce**
1 tbsp. **Vinegar**
1 tsp. **Lemon Juice**
2 tbsp. **Liquid Smoke**
1 1/2 tsp. **Soy Sauce**

3/4 tsp. **Dry Mustard**
2 tbsp. **Honey**
2 tbsp. **Brown Sugar**
1 tsp. **Accent®**
    (Monosodium Glutamate)
1 1/2 tsp. **Salt**
1/2 to 1 tsp. **Chili Powder**
4 cups **Hot Water**
Scant **Black Pepper**

Melt margarine and sauté onions. Add remaining ingredients and mix. Simmer one hour (or longer) until sauce is of desired consistency. Sauce may be frozen at this point. Makes six cups.

Note: to thicken sauce quickly, add two tablespoons cornstarch to two cups cold water. Add to sauce and cook until sauce thickens. DO NOT FREEZE AFTER CORNSTARCH HAS BEEN ADDED.

Jean's Barbecue Sauce

Jean Walters – La Mesa, California

1/2 bottle **Kraft®** or **Chris & Pitts®**
   Barbecue Sauce
2 to 3 tbsp. **Brown Sugar**
1 tsp. **Lemon Juice**

1/3 cup diced **Onion**
2 to 3 tbsp. **Syrup** or **Molasses**
1 tsp. **Sweet Hot Mustard**

Combine all ingredients and boil until thick, stirring constantly. Makes about one cup sauce.

"Suits Us" Barbecue Sauce

Gwendolyn B. Woodward – Rockport, Texas

1/2 cup **Wesson Oil**
1 cup chopped **Onion**
2 cloves **Garlic**, chopped
2 tbsp. **Brown Sugar**
1 tbsp. **Paprika**
1 tbsp. **Chili Powder**
1 tsp. **Salt**

1 tsp. **Dry Mustard**
1/8 tsp. **Cayenne Pepper**
1/4 cup **Vinegar**
1 can (8oz.) **Tomato Sauce**
1 cup **Water**
1/4 cup **Ketchup**
4 drops **Tabasco® Pepper Sauce**

Heat oil and sauté onion and garlic until transparent. Slowly add brown sugar, paprika, chili powder, salt, dry mustard and cayenne. Then add remaining ingredients slowly and simmer sauce on medium heat for one hour. Makes one pint.

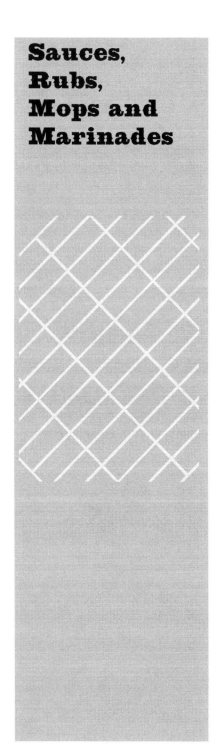

Weber® Tangy Barbecue Sauce

Courtesy Weber® – Stephen Products Co.

2 tbsp. **Butter** or **Margarine**
3 tbsp. chopped **Onion**
1/2 cup chopped **Celery**
2 tbsp. granulated **Sugar**
2 tbsp. **Vinegar**

1 tbsp. **Worcestershire Sauce**
1/4 cup **Lemon Juice**
1 tsp. **Dry Mustard**
1 cup **Ketchup**
Salt and **Pepper** to taste

Melt butter in a skillet. Sauté onions and celery until tender. Add remaining ingredients and cook about 15 to 20 minutes so flavors blend. Makes 1 1/2 cups sauce.

Texas-Style BBQ Sauce

Chef Franz Fershke – Phoenix, Az.

1 lb. **Mixed Pickling Spices**
2 **Whole Cloves**
14 oz. **Onions**, chopped
14 oz. **Celery**, chopped
72 oz. **Ketchup**
3/4 cup **Chili Sauce**
1/2 gal. **Water**
1/3 qt. **Cider Vinegar**

2 oz. **Coleman's® Mustard**
3/4 cup **Worcestershire Sauce**
10 oz. **Light Brown Sugar**
1/4 tbsp. **Garlic Powder**
1 1/2 oz. **Salt**
3/4 tsp. **Tabasco® Pepper Sauce**
1/8 cup **Lemon Juice**

Tie pickling spices and cloves loosely in cheesecloth bag. Combine all ingredients in heavy pot, heat to a boil, reduce heat and simmer slowly for about three hours. Remove from heat, cool partially. Remove spice bag. Pour mixture into blender and blend until smooth. Cover until ready to serve. Makes approximately one gallon.

Spicy Basting Sauce

Kikkoman® International, Inc.

1 cup **Orange Juice**
1/2 cup **Lemon Juice**
1/4 cup **Kikkoman® Soy Sauce**
1/4 cup packed **Brown Sugar**
1 tsp. **McCormick® or Schilling® Curry Powder**
1 tsp. **McCormick® or Schilling® Black Pepper**
1/2 tsp. **McCormick® or Schilling® Ginger**
1/4 tsp. **McCormick® or Schilling® Mace**

Combine all ingredients thoroughly. Use to baste turkeys or chickens during last 30 minutes of cooking. Makes 2 cups sauce.

Favorite BBQ Sauce

Mrs. Ollis Ford – Magnolia, Arkansas

1/2 cup **Wesson Oil**
1/2 cup **Onion**
1/2 cup **Celery**
1/2 cup **Green Pepper**
1 clove **Garlic**
2 tbsp. **Worcestershire Sauce**
2 tbsp. **Brown Sugar**
1 tsp. **Salt**

1/2 tsp. **Tabasco® Pepper Sauce**
1 cup **Ketchup**
1/2 cup **Vinegar**
1/4 tsp. **Chili Powder**
2 tsp. **Dry Mustard**
2 tsp. **Horseradish**
Juice of 1 **Lemon**

Chop (or grind) onions, celery and green pepper fine. Combine all ingredients, heat and simmer covered until all are tender. Makes enough sauce to baste 4 chicken or a dozen hamburgers.

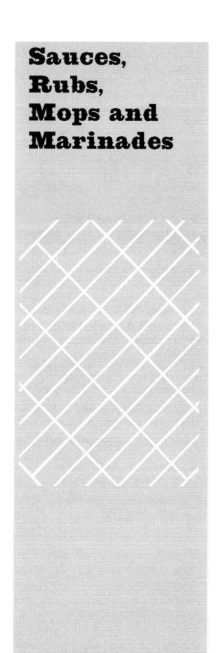

Carol's Home Made BarBQ Sauce

Carol Shock – Sidney, Ohio

1/4 cup **Vegetable Oil**
1 cup chopped fine **Onion**
1 tsp. **Garlic Salt**
3/4 cup **Water**
1/4 cup **Vinegar**
3 tbsp. **Worcestershire Sauce**

1 can (8 oz.) **Tomato Sauce**
1 cup **Ketchup**
2 cups **Sugar**
1 tsp. **Salt**
1 tsp. **Chili Powder**

Heat oil, add onion, and cook over low heat until onion is lightly browned. Add rest of ingredients and simmer 15 to 20 minutes. Makes about one quart.

Peanut Butter Barbeque Sauce

Judith B. Kinney – Richmond, Virginia

1 medium **Onion**
3 cloves **Garlic**
3 tbsp. **Peanut Oil**
1 1/2 cups **Creamy Peanut Butter**
1/2 cup **Brown Sugar**
1/4 cup **Lemon Juice**

1/4 cup **Orange Juice**
1/4 cup **Soy Sauce**
1/4 cup **Worcestershire Sauce**
1/2 cup **Beer**
Tabasco® **Pepper Sauce** to taste

Chop onion and garlic until almost liquid in food processor. Add peanut oil, peanut butter, brown sugar and process until smooth. (If food processor has a large mixing bowl, the entire mixture can be prepared in processor. Otherwise, at this point, scrape the mixture into a large bowl.) Add remaining ingredients and stir until well blended. Makes approx. 4 cups sauce that can be used as a marinade-basting sauce for ribs, pork or chicken.

Brenda's Blender BBQ Sauce

Brenda Glover – Tehuacana, Texas

1/2 cup **Liquid Smoke**
2 cups **Ketchup**
1/4 cup **Yellow Mustard**
2 tbsp. **Chili Powder**

1/4 tsp. **Garlic Powder**
1/4 tsp. **Celery Salt**
1/4 tsp. **Ground Oregano**
1 tsp. **Salt**

Combine first four ingredients in a blender, and blend for one minute at slow speed. Add last four ingredients and blend at higher speed until thoroughly mixed. Pour into quart jar and refrigerate. Makes 2 3/4 cups sauce. For more robust flavor, make sauce a day before using.

Frank's Barbecue Sauce

Frank J. Arkell, Jr. – Scottsdale, Arizona

3 tbsp. **Open Pit® Barbecue Sauce**
1/2 cup **Hunt's® Ketchup**
3 tbsp. **Kraft® Sweet & Sour Sauce**
2 tbsp. **Dark Brown Sugar**
1/4 tsp. **Chili Powder**
1/2 tsp. **Salt**
1/4 tsp. fresh **Ground Pepper**
1/2 tsp. **Soy Sauce**

1/4 cup chopped **Onion**
4 cloves **Garlic**, minced
1 tsp. **Celery Seed**
1/4 cup **Red Wine**
1/2 tsp. **Basil**
Dash **Ginger**
Pinch **Anise Seed**

Combine ingredients in saucepan and heat until boiling. Turn heat down and simmer 5 to 10 minutes. Spoon over spareribs on grill. Keep remaining sauce warm and serve with ribs at table. Makes two cups sauce, enough for 3 lbs. ribs.

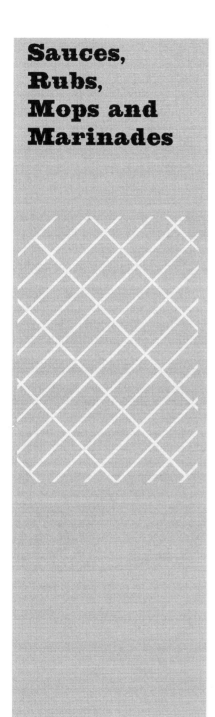

"Doug's Kickoff" Barbecue Sauce

D. E. Davis – Holly Hill, Florida

2 cups **Ketchup**
1 cup table **Mustard**
1/3 cup **Worcestershire Sauce**
1 tbsp. **Curry Powder**

1 tbsp. **Liquid Smoke**
1 tsp. **Cumin Powder**
1 tsp. **Tabasco® Pepper Sauce**
1/2 cup **Honey** or **Syrup**

Mix all ingredients well (DO NOT COOK). Taste test with tip of index finger. For additional "kick" add one tablespoon Tabasco® Pepper Sauce. Paint sauce generously on ribs, pork, beef or chicken. (Sauce for 20 servings)

Hot Barbecue Sauce

Earl E. Ellman – St. Louis, Missouri

1 cup fresh **Lemon Juice**
2/3 cup **Apple Cider Vinegar**
2/3 cup unsalted **Tomato Juice**
1/2 cup **Water**
3 tbsp. **Brown Sugar**
2 tsp. **Garlic Powder**
2 tsp. **Dry Mustard**

2 tsp. **Paprika**
1 tsp. **Ground Black Pepper**
1 tsp. **Ground Red Pepper**
1 tsp. **Onion Powder**
2 tsp. **Red Hot Sauce**
1/4 cup **Saffron Oil**

Combine all ingredients together in a saucepan. Heat to boiling point. Remove from heat and use for barbecuing meat or poultry. Makes approximately three cups sauce.

Mosley's Barbecue Sauce

Margaret E. Mosley – Bearden, Arkansas

1/2 gallon **Vinegar**
1/2 gallon **Orange Juice**
1/2 gallon **Tomato Juice**
Juice of 1 **Lemon**
1 jar (6 oz.) **Mustard**

5 cans (6 oz. each) **Tomato Paste**
6 cans (2.4 oz. each) **Chili Powder**
1/2 cup **Salt**
4 cups **Sugar**
Red Pepper to taste

Mix above ingredients thoroughly and cook about two hours (or until thickened). Use with cooked pork, beef, chicken, with beans, or in casseroles. Makes approx. 10-12 pints.

Table Barbecue Sauce

Mrs. Johnnie Davis – Tallahassee, Florida

1 cup **Ketchup**
1/2 cup **Cider Vinegar**
1 tsp. **Sugar**
1 tsp. **Chili Powder**
1/8 tsp. **Salt**
1 1/2 cups **Water**
3 ribs **Celery**, chopped

3 **Bay Leaves**
1 clove **Garlic**
2 tbsp. chopped **Onion**
4 tbsp. **Butter**
4 tbsp. **Worcestershire Sauce**
1 tsp. **Paprika**
Dash **Black Pepper**

Combine all ingredients and bring to a boil. Simmer about fifteen minutes. Remove from heat and strain. This recipe may be refrigerated up to two weeks before using. Makes 2 1/2 cups sauce.

Barbecue Sauce with Mushrooms

Mike Padgett – San Diego, California

3/4 cup **Onion**
3/4 cup **Celery**
1/2 cup **Mushrooms**
1/4 cup **Oil**
1/2 cup **Brown Sugar**
1 tbsp. plus 1 tsp. **Mustard**

1 tsp. **Salt**
1 tbsp. plus 1 tsp. **Worcestershire Sauce**
2 tbsp. **Cider Vinegar**
1 1/4 cups **Water**

Mince the onions, celery and mushrooms. Heat oil in a saucepan. Add minced vegetables and sauté without browning. Add remaining ingredients, stir, and simmer for 30 minutes. Stir occasionally, or until thickened. Makes one quart of sauce.

Golden Grill Barbecue Sauce

Glenda McGillis – Phoenix, Arizona

1/4 cup **Sugar**
2 tbsp. **Cornstarch**
1/2 tsp. **Allspice**
1/2 tsp. **Ground Cloves**

1 cup fresh **Orange Juice**
2 tbsp. **Vinegar**
4 tbsp. **Butter** or **Margarine**

Combine sugar, cornstarch, allspice and cloves in a small saucepan. Slowly stir in orange juice and vinegar. Stir constantly over medium heat until sauce thickens. Boil for three minutes. Stir in butter. Makes one cup sauce.

Smoky BBQ Sauce

Lorraine Nunemaker – San Bruno, Californa

1/2 cup **Vinegar**
1/2 cup **Ketchup**
1/3 cup **Water**
3 tbsp. **Worcestershire Sauce**
1/2 tsp. **Salt**
1/8 tsp. **Tabasco® Pepper Sauce**
3 tbsp. **Brown Sugar**
2 tsp. **Dry Mustard**
3 tbsp. **Chianti Wine**

1 tbsp. **Chili Powder**
1/2 cup **Tomato Juice**
3 tbsp. minced **Onion**
1/4 tsp. **Garlic Powder**
1 tbsp. **Paprika**
1 **Bay Leaf**
2 tsp. **Liquid Smoke**
Dash of **Celery Salt**
Coarse **Ground Pepper** to taste

Combine all ingredients in a saucepan. Bring to a boil. Simmer, uncovered, for one hour. Makes enough sauce for 5 to 6 lbs. ribs.

Grandma's Old Fashion Barbecue Sauce

Shalane Marie Carmouche – Cottonport, La.

6 large diced **Onions**
1 jar (8 oz.) **Cooking Oil**
6 cans (8 oz.) **Hunt's Tomato Sauce**
1 stick (1/4-lb.) **Butter**
2 tsp. **Mustard**
1 1/2 tbsp. **Mayonnaise**

1 bottle (14 oz.) **Ketchup**
1 bottle (18 oz.) **Kraft® Barbecue Sauce**
25-30 drops **Tabasco® Pepper Sauce**
3 cups **Sugar**

Heat cooking oil and add onions until smothered. Next, add tomato sauce and let simmer three minutes. Then add remaining ingredients EXCEPT sugar. Let mixture cook five minutes, then add sugar gradually, stirring constantly. Lower heat and cook (covered) slowly, about one to two hours. Sauce can also be used over spaghetti.

Molly's Favorite BBQ Sauce

Molly Hatch – Memphis, Tennessee

2 tbsp. **Oil**
1 **Onion**, chopped
1 cup **Ketchup**
1/2 cup **Water**

1/4 cup **Brown Sugar**
3 tbsp. **Worcestershire Sauce**
1 tbsp. **Salt**
1/4 tsp. **Garlic Powder**

Heat oil in saucepan and sauté onion until tender. Add remaining ingredients, stir, and simmer covered for about 8 to 10 minutes. Makes 2 cups sauce.

Betty's Barbeque Sauce

Betty Smith – Biscoe, Arkansas

2 tbsp. **Butter**
1 medium **Onion**
1 clove **Garlic**, minced
3/4 cup **Water**
1 cup **Ketchup**
2 tbsp. **Vinegar**

2 tbsp. **Lemon Juice**
2 tbsp. **Worcestershire Sauce**
2 tbsp. **Brown Sugar**
1 tsp. **Dry Mustard**
1 tsp. **Salt**
1/4 tsp. **Black Pepper**

Slice onions. Melt butter in saucepan, add onions, and heat until tender. Add remaining ingredients and cook slowly for 20 minutes. Makes about 2 1/4 cups.

Filomena's Favorite Sauce

Bonnie Proctor – Big Spring, Texas

1 medium **Onion**
2 tbsp. **Butter** or **Margarine**
1 bottle (12 oz.) **Chili Sauce**
1 cup **Brown Sugar**

2 tbsp. **Paprika**
2 tbsp. **Worcestershire Sauce**
1/4 tsp. **Garlic Salt**
Juice of 1 large **Lemon**

Chop onion fine. Melt butter in saucepan, add onions and simmer until soft (but not brown). Add remaining ingredients EXCEPT lemon juice, mix well, and cook on low heat, stirring occasionally for 20 minutes. Remove from heat, and squeeze lemon juice into mixture. Sauce is ready at this point, but is better if allowed to stand for 30 minutes before using. Makes one quart. Sauce is very sweet, tastes best on chicken, pork or hamburgers, but is NOT recommended for steaks.

Max's Famous Barbecue Sauce

Max D. Smith – Tucson, Arizona

3 tbsp. **Butter**
1/4 cup **Vinegar**
1 tbsp. **Lemon Juice**
1 medium **Onion**, grated
1 cup **Ketchup**
1/2 cup **Water**
2 tbsp. **Brown Sugar**
2 tsp. **Dry Mustard**

2 tbsp. **Worcestershire Sauce**
1 tsp. **Salt**
1 tbsp. **Paprika**
1/4 tsp. **Chili Powder**
6 tbsp. **Chili Sauce**
1/8 tsp. **Red Pepper**
1/8 tsp. **Cayenne Pepper**

Combine all ingredients in a large saucepan and simmer for 15 minutes. Makes about one quart.

Sauces, Rubs, Mops and Marinades

Butter Barbecue Sauce

Courtesy American Dairy Association

1/2 cup (1 stick) **Butter**
1/2 cup chopped **Onion**
1/2 cup **Ketchup**
1/4 cup firmly packed **Light
Brown Sugar**

3 tbsp. **Worcestershire Sauce**
1 1/2 tsp. **Chili Powder**
1 tsp. **Salt**
1/8 tsp. **Pepper**
Dash **Tabasco® Pepper Sauce**

Melt butter in saucepan. Add onion and sauté until tender. Stir in remaining ingredients and simmer five minutes. Sauce will store well in refrigerator, but should be warmed before using. Ideal for hamburgers. Makes one cup.

Dorothy's BBQ Sauce

Dorothy Pike – Lexington Park, Maryland

1 cup chopped **Onions**
1/3 cup **Oil**
3 tbsp. **Brown Sugar**
4 tsp. **Dry Mustard**
1 tsp. **Salt**
1/2 tsp. **Black Pepper**
3 tsp. **Chili Powder**

2 cloves **Garlic**
1 1/2 cups **Ketchup**
1 cup **Water**
3/4 cup **Vinegar**
3 tsp. **Worcestershire Sauce**
Few drops **Hot Pepper Sauce**

Heat oil and sauté onions. Add remaining ingredients and simmer for 15 minutes. Makes one quart.

Martha's BBQ Sauce

Martha Helton – Perry, Florida

2 slices **Lemon**
2 tsp. **Lemon Juice**
1/4 lb. **Butter**, **Margarine** or
　Cooking Oil of choice
1 cup **Cider Vinegar**
1 **Onion**, minced
1/2 cup **Water**

1 clove **Garlic**
2 tbsp. **Mustard**
3 tbsp. **Sugar**
1 tbsp. **Worcestershire Sauce**
2 tbsp. **Ketchup**
2 tbsp. **Chili Powder**
1/2 pod **Red Pepper**

Combine all ingredients and heat to boiling point. Baste meat with sauce until meat is completely cooked. This sauce is especially good if used on a Boston butt pork roast cooked over charcoal fire.

Texas Style Barbecue Sauce

Margaret A. Allen – Marlin, Texas

1/2 stick **Margarine**
1 medium **Onion**, finely chopped
1 bottle (12 oz.) **Chili Sauce**
1 cup canned, chopped **Tomatoes**
2 cups **Tomato Juice**
1 bottle (14 oz.) **Ketchup**

2 tbsp. **Worcestershire Sauce**
1/2 tsp. **Garlic Powder**
2 tbsp. **Sugar**
Salt and **Pepper** to taste
1/4 cup **Cider Vinegar**

Heat margarine in saucepan and sauté onion. Add remaining ingredients EXCEPT vinegar. Simmer thirty minutes. Add vinegar and simmer ten minutes longer. Makes a quart and a half sauce. Fresh tomatoes may be substituted for canned, but sauce should be used immediately and not stored.

Pork Chop Barbecue Sauce

Jane E. Cotton – Little Rock, Arkansas

1/2 cup finely chopped **Onion**	1 tsp. **Salt**
1 can **Tomato Paste**	1 tsp. **Paprika**
3/4 cup **Water**	1 tsp. **Chili Powder**
4 tbsp. **Wine Vinegar**	Dash **Black Pepper**
2 tbsp. **Brown Sugar**	Dash **Cinnamon**, optional
2 tbsp. **Worcestershire Sauce**	Dash **Cloves**, optional
2 tbsp. **Ketchup**	

Combine all ingredients and simmer until well blended. Pour over six pork chops and bake in 300 degree oven one hour.

Marcia's Ol' Fashion Barbecue Sauce

Marcia Cernoch – Rosenberg, Texas

1/4 lb. **Butter**	4 cups **Ketchup**
3 cloves **Garlic**, minced	1 can (46 oz.) **Tomato Juice**
1 **Onion**, chopped	1/4 cup **Chili Powder**
1 **Lemon**, diced	1/4 cup **Vinegar**
1/2 cup **Worcestershire Sauce**	1 can (46 oz.) **V-8 Juice**
1/2 cup **Brown Sugar**	**Salt** and **Pepper** to taste

Heat butter, and sauté garlic, onion and diced lemon (rind and pulp). Add remaining ingredients and simmer all together a couple of hours until sauce thickens. Makes about four gallons.

Kay's Bar-B-Q Sauce

Kay Lindsey – Monette, Arkansas

1/4 cup chopped **Onion**
3 tbsp. **Butter**
1 cup **Ketchup**
1/3 cup **Vinegar**
1 cup **Brown Sugar**

1/4 cup **Water**
2 tbsp. **Mustard**
1 tbsp. **Worcestershire Sauce**
1/2 tsp. **Salt**
1/8 tsp. **Black Pepper**

Heat butter in saucepan and add onions, cooking until tender. Add remaining ingredients. Cover and simmer for 30 minutes. Makes enough sauce for 4 lbs. spare ribs or a 4-lb. chicken.

Ella's Barbecue Sauce

Ella Flora – Rocky Mount, North Carolina

1/2 cup **Vinegar**
2 tbsp. **Mustard**
1 tsp. **Black Pepper**
Crushed **Red Pepper** to taste
Dash **Sugar**
1 tbsp. **Soy Sauce**
1 cup **Ketchup**

1 cup **Water**
1/2 tsp. **Garlic Salt**
1/2 tsp. **Salt**
1 tbsp. **Lemon Juice**
1 **Onion**, chopped
4 tbsp. **Worcestershire Sauce**

Combine all ingredients EXCEPT ketchup and Worcestershire Sauce. Simmer for 20 minutes on low heat. Add ketchup and Worcestershire Sauce. Bring to a boil and boil for one minute. Makes 2 1/2 cups.

Cattle Ranch Bar-B-Que Sauce

Dian Broening – Scottsdale, Arizona

1/2 lb. **Butter**	2 or 3 **Onions**, ground
1/2 cup **Vinegar**	1 bottle (10 oz.) **Worcestershire Sauce**
1/2 lb. **Bacon Grease**	1 bottle (24 oz.) **Ketchup**
or 1 cup **Wesson Oil**	1 tbsp. **Salt**
1 tbsp. **Black Pepper**	1 tbsp. **Celery Salt**
1 tbsp. **Red (Cayenne) Pepper**	1 tsp. **Garlic Salt**

Combine all ingredients and simmer on very low fire for at least 20 minutes. Makes sauce for 25 lbs. of meat. Excellent for spareribs.

Steak Barbecue Sauce

Mary L. Gough – Reedville, Virginia

1 tbsp. **Salt**	1/2 tsp. **Onion Powder**
1 tbsp. **Black Pepper**	or 1 tbsp. grated **Onion**
1 tsp. **Dry Mustard**	1/2 tsp. **Red Pepper**
1 tbsp. **Tabasco® Pepper Sauce**	2 tbsp. **Parmesan Cheese**
2 tbsp. **Garlic Powder**	1/3 cup **Worcestershire Sauce**
	1/4 cup **Heinz® 57 Sauce**

Combine all ingredients and stir until well mixed. One-half hour before grilling, brush both sides of 3-lb. steak (or hamburger).

Immediately before cooking, brush meat again. Meat can be broiled in oven or cooked on grill. If desired, brush again with sauce during broiling.

Mom's North Carolina Barbecue Sauce

Joyce Wells – Danville, Virginia

1 quart **Vinegar**	2 tbsp. **Cumin Seed**
1/4 lb. (1 stick) **Butter**	2 tbsp. **Dry Mustard**
1 (10 oz.) bottle **Worcestershire Sauce**	2 tbsp. **Paprika**
1 tbsp. **Soy Sauce**	2 tbsp. **Chili Powder**
1 tbsp. **Black Pepper**	2 **Bay Leaves**
1 tbsp. **Cayenne Pepper**	1 tbsp. **Salt**

Combine all ingredients and boil for five minutes. Remove bay leaves. Makes five to six cups sauce.

Barbecue Basting Sauce

Reprinted from *Barbequed Chicken* by Robert C. Baker by permission of Cornell Cooperative Extension and NYS College of Agriculture and Life Science.

1 **Egg**	3 tbsp. **Salt**
1 cup **Cooking Oil**	1 tbsp. **Poultry Seasoning**
1 pint **Cider Vinegar**	1 tsp. **Pepper**

Beat the egg, then add the oil and beat again. Add remaining ingredients and stir.

This recipe makes enough sauce for 10 broiler halves, weighing about one pound each. Brush sauce on broiler halves every few minutes with a fiber brush. To reduce quantity of sauce in half, divide ingredients by two, except for egg and salt. Use a whole egg and two tablespoons of salt. Leftover sauce can be refrigerated in a tightly covered glass jar for several weeks.

Tennessee Barbecue Sauce

Courtesy: Jack Daniel's® Charcoal

1 medium **Onion**, finely chopped
1 clove **Garlic**, minced
2 tbsp. **Vegetable Oil**
1 1/2 cups **Ketchup**
1/4 cup **Brown Sugar**

2 tbsp. **Jack Daniel's® Whiskey**
1 tsp. **Liquid Smoke**
2 1/2 tbsp. **Cider Vinegar**
1/2 tsp. **Dry Mustard**
2 drops **Hot Pepper Sauce**

Sauté onion and garlic in vegetable oil until tender. Stir in remaining ingredients and bring to a boil over medium heat. Reduce heat and simmer for 10 minutes. Makes about two cups. Ideal for chicken, pork and beef.

Cowpoke Barbecue Sauce

Glenda McGillis – Phoenix, Arizona

1/4 cup **Brown Sugar**
1/4 cup **Salad Oil**
2 tsp. **Salt**
1 tsp. **Garlic Powder**
1 cup **Vinegar**

3/4 cup fresh **Lemon Juice**
2 cups **Water**
1 bottle (5 oz.) **Worcestershire Sauce**
Dash of **Tabasco® Pepper Sauce**

Combine all ingredients in saucepan. Bring quickly to boiling point. Reduce heat and simmer ten minutes. Cool and pour into one-quart container. Will keep refrigerated several weeks.

Tip: Generally speaking, sauces which contain any form of sugar or tomatoes should not be used to baste or barbeque meats since both burn easily. Instead, serve such sauces with the meat.

Basic Teriyaki Sauce

Kikkoman® International, Inc.

1/2 cup **Kikkoman® Soy Sauce**
1/4 **White Wine**
2 tbsp. **Sugar**
1/2 tsp. **McCormick®** or **Schilling® Ginger**
1/4 tsp. **McCormick®** or **Schilling® Garlic Powder**

Blend together all ingredients, stirring until sugar dissolves. Use as marinade for steaks or chicken, or brush on meat during grilling. Makes 3/4 cup sauce.

Arni's Barbecue Sauce

Arni Munson – North Little Rock, Arkansas

2 cups **Ketchup**
1/2 cup **Reconstituted Lemon Juice**
1/2 cup firmly packed **Brown Sugar**
1/2 cup **Mustard**
1/2 cup finely chopped **Onion**
1/4 cup **Butter** or **Margarine**
1/4 cup **Worcestershire Sauce**
1 clove **Garlic**, finely chopped
1/4 tsp. **Salt**
1/8 tsp. **Tabasco® Pepper Sauce** (or any hot sauce)

Combine all ingredients in saucepan. Simmer (with cover on) for twenty minutes, stirring occasionally. After pork or chicken is almost done, pour sauce over meat and simmer in oven on 300 degrees for approximately 45 minutes. Sauce can also be brushed on when using outdoor grill. Makes one quart.

All Purpose Barbecue Sauce

Courtesy Best Foods – New Jersey

2 tbsp. **Corn Oil**
1/4 cup finely chopped **Onion**
1 cup **Chili Sauce**
1/3 cup **Water**

1/4 cup **Karo® Dark Corn Syrup**
1/4 cup **Cider Vinegar**
1 tbsp. **Worcestershire Sauce**
1/2 tsp. **Salt**

In a 1 1/2-quart saucepan, heat corn oil over medium heat. Add onion and sauté five minutes. Stir in remaining ingredients. Bring to a boil. Reduce heat and simmer ten minutes. Remove from heat. Brush on meats or poultry during last twenty minutes of cooking. Makes two cups.

Lane Bar-B-Que Sauce

Betty Thomas – Little Rock, Arkansas

1/4 cup **Brown Sugar**
1/2 cup **Ketchup**
1/3 cup **Vinegar**
4 tbsp. **Oil**
1/4 cup **Water**

2 tbsp. **Worcestershire Sauce**
1/2 tsp. **Salt**
1/2 cup **Molasses**
1/2 tsp. **Garlic Powder**
4 tbsp. **Chili Powder**

Combine all ingredients in saucepan and bring to a boil. Simmer five minutes, stirring often. Makes one pint of sauce.

Tip: NEVER spray a fire with fluid AFTER it has been lit, since the fluid may flash up.

Loris' BBQ Sauce

Loris Marshall – Colorado City, Texas

2 cups **Ketchup**
2 cups **Vinegar**
1/4 tsp. **Tabasco® Pepper Sauce**
2 cloves **Garlic**, minced
1 cup **Sugar**

1 tbsp. **Worcestershire Sauce**
2 tsp. **Dry Mustard**
1 1/2 tbsp. **Salt**
2 tsp. **Liquid Smoke**

Combine all ingredients in heavy pot and simmer about ten minutes. Makes one quart.

Un-Secret BBQ Sauce

Liz Van Brunt – Wickenburg, Arizona

1/3 cup **Ketchup**
1/6 cup **Vinegar**
1 **Onion**, chopped
1 tbsp. **Paprika**
1 tsp. **Chili Powder**

1 tsp. **Salt**
1/2 tsp. **Garlic Powder**
1/2 tsp. **Black Pepper**
2 tbsp. **Liquid Smoke** (a Must)

Simmer all ingredients about half an hour. Spoon over barbecue or, at home, over sliced roast beef or pork.

Sauces, Rubs, Mops and Marinades

Tip: Lighter fluids should be kept out of direct sunlight and other hot locations.

Joan's Original BBQ Sauce

Joan Cordiero – Davidsonville, Maryland

1 can (51 oz.) **Orange Juice**
1 can (51 oz.) **Grapefruit Juice**
1/2 cup **Vinegar**
1/2 cup **Brown Sugar**
2 tbsp. **Cloves**
2 tbsp. **Dry Mustard**
2 tbsp. **Ginger**
2 tbsp. **Maple Syrup**

1 to 2 cups **Wine** (Red or White)
1 tbsp. **Garlic Salt**
4 tbsp. **Soy Sauce**
2 cans (28 oz.) **Mandarin Oranges**, fruit and juice
1 can (28 oz.) **Sliced Peaches**, fruit and juice
1 can (18 oz.) **Maraschino Cherries**, fruit and juice

Mix all ingredients thoroughly in a large cooking pan. Bring to a boil and simmer approximately one hour. Marinate meat in this sauce for about 24 hours, using a covered dish, turning meat occasionally. Baste with sauce while grilling. Sauce is slightly sweet and sour. (Do not use frozen orange or grapefruit juice.) Marinate chicken about four hours, covered, refrigerated, turning at least once. Baste with sauce while barbecuing. Marinate pork chops and spareribs eight to ten hours (or overnight), covered, refrigerated, turning occasionally. Makes approximately two gallons sauce.

Note: Fruits and juices may be changed for variation. However, always include one large can orange juice.

Tip: After coals have reached the desired temperature, arrange them in a single layer directly under the food for direct cooking.

Vida's Barbecue Sauce

Vida L. Kaplan – Naranja, Florida

1 **Onion**, peeled and cut
2 cloves **Garlic**
1 1/2 tsp. **Mustard**
1 tsp. **Salt**

1 1/2 tsp. **Chili Powder**
1 cup **Tomato Sauce** or **Tomato Soup**
4 tbsp. **Vinegar** or **Lime Juice**
1/2 cup **Water**

Place all ingredients in blender and blend until well chopped. Marinate meat or chicken in sauce about three hours before cooking and baste while cooking. Makes about two cups sauce.

Sweet and Sour Polynesian Sauce

By Permission Lea & Perrins®, Inc.

1/2 cup **Pineapple Juice**
1/4 cup **Honey**
3 tbsp. Lea & Perrins®
   Worcestershire Sauce

1 1/2 tsp. **Ginger**
1 tsp. **Salt**
1/2 tsp. **Garlic Powder**

Combine all ingredients and use to brush over ribs, chicken or pork during last 15 minutes of cooking. Makes one cup sauce.

Tip: Never move outdoor barbecues into a garage or other closed area if it rains. Within minutes, smoldering charcoal can build up deadly concentrations of carbon monoxide. Even with an open window, the fumes are toxic.

Betty's Best BBQ Sauce

Betty Shaw – Santee, California

1 cup **Ketchup**
4 tsp. **Mustard**
2 tbsp. **Cider Vinegar**
4 tsp. **Hot Sauce**

1/4 cup packed **Brown Sugar**
1 tsp. **Garlic Powder**
2 tbsp. **Liquid Smoke**
2 tbsp. **Worcestershire Sauce**

Combine all ingredients and simmer on medium heat for 10 minutes.

Corn Starch Barbecue Sauce

Courtesy Best Foods – New Jersey

2 tbsp. **Argo® Corn Starch**
1/4 cup **Vinegar**
2/3 cup **Karo® Dark Corn Syrup**
1/3 cup **Soy Sauce**

1 1/2 tsp. **Ginger**
1 clove **Garlic**, crushed
1/4 tsp. **Salt**
Dash **Pepper**

Combine corn starch and vinegar in a saucepan. Stir in remaining ingredients and bring to a boil, stirring occasionally. This sauce is excellent on spareribs.

Tip: All flammable objects should be kept away from the fire.

Shiny Citrus Sauce

Kikkoman® International, Inc.

1 cup **Water**
1/2 cup **Kikkoman® Soy Sauce**
1/4 cup **Lime Marmalade**

3 tbsp. **Cornstarch**
1/4 cup **Water**
1 1/2 tsp. grated **Lemon Rind**

Bring water, soy sauce and marmalade to boil over medium heat. Stir until marmalade dissolves. Combine cornstarch with water. Add to sauce mixture and cook until sauce thickens. Stir in lemon rind. Makes 2 cups sauce to serve over grilled fish.

Zesty Bar-B-Q Sauce

1 cup **Ketchup**
1 1/2 cups **Water**
1/4 cup **Brown Sugar**
1/4 cup **Vinegar**
2 tbsp. **Worcestershire Sauce**

1 tsp. **Celery Salt**
1 tsp. **Chili Powder**
1/4 tsp. **Pepper**
Dash **Hot Pepper Sauce**
1 to 2 tbsp. **Flour**

Mix all ingredients in saucepan on low heat for ten minutes. Stir frequently. Makes about two cups.

Tip: A grill thermometer placed directly on the cooking grill is a reliable index of the temperature of the coals.

Jose's Barbecue Sauce

Josephine S. Young – Gardena, California

1 can (8 oz.) **Tomato Sauce**
1/4 cup **Dark Brown Sugar**
4 tbsp. **Cider Vinegar**
1/4 tsp. **Cinnamon**

1 tbsp. **Worcestershire Sauce**
1 tbsp. **Liquid Smoke**
Dash of **Cloves**
Dash of **Allspice**

Combine all ingredients and bring to a boil. Simmer about 30 minutes. Makes a little over one cup sauce.

Southwestern Barbecue Sauce

Kikkoman® International, Inc.

1 cup **Ketchup**
1/2 cup **Kikkoman® Soy Sauce**
1/4 cup packed **Brown Sugar**
1/4 cup **Vinegar**

1 tsp. **McCormick®** or
  Schilling® Chili Powder
1/4 tsp. **Tabasco® Pepper Sauce**
1/8 tsp. **Liquid Smoke**

Combine all ingredients in saucepan. Bring to boil, reduce heat and simmer five minutes. Use to brush chicken or ribs during last 15 minutes of cooking time. Makes 2 cups sauce.

Chicken Bar-B-Q Sauce

Mrs. Dayle C. Baker – Grand Ridge, Florida

1 jar **Horseradish Mustard**
1/2 lb. **Margarine**
1 cup **Vinegar**
1 heaping tbsp. **Salt**

1/2 bottle **Worcestershire Sauce**
1 tbsp. **Chili Powder**
1 cup **Water**

Combine all ingredients, heat and bring to a boil. This sauce is adequate for ten chicken halves.

Lemon Bar-B-Q Sauce for Fish

Josephine S. Young – Gardena, California

1/2 cup **Lemon Juice**
1/4 cup **Salad Oil**
2 tbsp. grated **Onion**
1/2 tsp. **Salt**

1/2 tsp. **Black Pepper**
1 tsp. **Dry Mustard**
2 tbsp. **Brown Sugar**
Dash of **Tabasco® Pepper Sauce**

Mix ingredients well, stirring until sugar is dissolved. Makes enough sauce for one pound fish fillets.

Seasoning & Sauce for Texas Barbecued Ribs

Mr. & Mrs. Johnnie Davis – Tallahasee, Florida

Dry Seasoning

3 tbsp. **Salt**

3 tbsp. **Sugar**

1 1/4 tbsp. **Black Pepper**

1 1/2 tsp. **Paprika**

1 1/2 tsp. **Dry Lemon Powder**
(unsweetened Kool-Aid®)

Mix together all dry seasoning ingredients and sprinkle ribs on both sides with mixture. Then baste with sauce.

Basting Sauce

1/2 tsp. **Salt**

1 tsp. **Dry Mustard**

1 clove **Garlic**, crushed

1/2 small **Bay Leaf**

1/3 tsp. **Chili Powder**

1/2 tsp. **Paprika**

3/4 tsp. **Hot Pepper Sauce**

1/2 cup **Worcestershire Sauce**

1/4 cup **Cider Vinegar**

2 cups **Beef Stock** or
Canned Beef Bouillon

1/4 cup **Vegetable Oil**

Combine all ingredients. Grill ribs slowly, basting often with sauce. This sauce will keep several days in refrigerator and can be frozen.

If ribs are cut into serving pieces, the sauce will baste eight pounds of ribs.

Tip: Never barbecue under a tree, since sparks can ignite the leaves and start a fire.

Recaito Sauce a la Goya

Original recipe created by Master Chef Felipe Rojas Lombardi expressly for the Goya Foods, Inc. *Latin Barbecue a la Goya Cookbook.* All rights reserved.

1/2 cup **Goya® Extra-Virgin Spanish Olive Oil**
2 large cloves **Garlic**, finely minced
1 cup finely chopped **Onion**
2 tbsp. finely chopped fresh **Ginger**
2 tbsp. **Goya® Hot Sauce**
4 tbsp. **Goya® Recaito**
1/4 cup **Water**
2 tbsp. **Lemon Juice**
1/4 tsp. **White Pepper**
1 tsp. **Sugar**
1/2 cup finely chopped **Coriander Leaves**
1/2 cup **La Vina White Cooking Wine**

Heat oil in saucepan, sauté garlic and ginger until golden. Add onions and sauté until translucent. Stir in other ingredients and simmer ten minutes. This is salsa for fish. Makes two cups.

Note: Goya® Recaito is a puree of fresh green peppers, onions, garlic and fresh coriander, an authentic spice and condiment mixture distinctively Latin in taste.

Tip: Wood chips and chunks are commonly used to impart flavor during grilling. Chips are thin pieces of wood about two inches wide and an inch thick. Since chips may produce sparks when added directly to briquettes, they are ideal for gas grills. Wood chunks are used most frequently with charcoal fires.

Jack Daniel's® Marinade

Courtesy Jack Daniel's® Charcoal

1/2 cup **Pineapple Juice**
3 tbsp. **Soy Sauce**
1 1/2 tsp. **Ginger**

1/2 tsp. **Garlic Powder**
1/4 cup **Jack Daniel's® Whiskey**

Combine ingredients and mix well. Dip meat in sauce and place on grill over hot coals. When meat is turned, brush with sauce. Grill to desired doneness. Just before meat is removed from grill, brush with sauce again. Makes 8 servings.

Hawaiian Island Marinade

Hawaii Ginger Industry Association

1/3 cup **Soy Sauce**
2 tbsp. **Lime Juice**
1 tbsp. **Honey**

2 tbsp. finely grated fresh
Hawaiian Ginger Root

Combine ingredients and marinate steak, ribs, chicken, fish or pork before barbequing. Baste with marinade during barbequing.

Tip: To avoid being burnt from dropped embers, wear closed shoes when barbecuing.

Chicken Marinade

Courtesy Weber® – Stephen Products Co.

1/2 cup **Soy Sauce**
1/4 cup **Vegetable Oil**
1/4 cup **Red Wine Vinegar**
1 tsp. **Oregano**

1/2 tsp. **Sweet Basil**
1/2 tsp. **Garlic Powder with Parsley**
1/4 tsp. **Black Pepper**

Combine all ingredients. Pour over chicken pieces in a non-metal dish. Cover and refrigerate overnight, turning pieces occasionally. Use marinade to baste chicken while barbecuing.

Bourbon Marinade

Marilyn A. Sorensen – Saugus, California

1/4 cup **Bourbon**
1/4 cup **Soy Sauce**
1/4 cup **Dijon Mustard**
1/4 cup **Brown Sugar**

1 small **Onion**, chopped fine
1/4 tsp. **Garlic Powder**
Dash **Worcestershire Sauce**

Combine all ingredients in a small bowl, mix well and refrigerate. Use this marinade on all types of meat, chicken, fish, vegetables, etc. Makes one cup.

Tip: Dry seasonings are rubbed on before grilling; marinades are used before and during cooking; sauces are brushed on just before cooking is completed.

Lemon-Rosemary Rub

1 1/2 tsp. grated **Lemon Peel**
1 tsp. crushed **Dried Rosemary Leaves**
1/4 tsp. **Salt**
1/4 tsp. dried **Thyme Leaves**
1/4 tsp. **Coarse Ground Black Pepper**
2 large cloves **Garlic**, minced

Combine all ingredients and use to season tender beef steaks or roasts. Makes enough to season two pounds of beef.

Southwestern Rub

1 1/2 tsp. **Chili Powder**
1 tsp. **Garlic Powder**
1/2 tsp. crushed **Dried Oregano Leaves**
1/4 tsp. **Ground Cumin**

Combine all ingredients. Use to season tender beef steaks or roasts. Makes enough to season two pounds of beef.

Note: Rubs are applied to the exterior surfaces of the meat just before grilling. They need no standing time. For convenience, rubs may be applied several hours in advance and the coated meat then refrigerated until grilling time. Flavors become more pronounced the longer the rub is on the meat. (These recipes courtesy the National Live Stock and Meat Board)

Dry Rib Seasoning

Walter Jetton's LBJ Barbecue Cook Book (Courtesy Simon & Schuster)

6 tbsp. **Salt**	2 tbsp. **MSG** (or other pep powder)
6 tbsp. **Sugar**	2 1/2 tbsp. **Black Pepper**
1 tbsp. **Dry Lemon Powder**	1 tbsp. **Paprika**

This recipe is for sprinkling on spareribs before barbecuing. Use heaping measures when mixing ingredients, and do not skimp when sprinkling on ribs.

Makes about 12 ounces of seasoning.

Soy Glaze for Ribs

4 tbsp. **Soy Sauce**	3 drops **Tabasco® Pepper Sauce**
1/4 tsp. fresh **Ground Black Pepper**	1 3/4 cups **Honey**

Combine soy sauce, pepper, and Tabasco®, and spread over spareribs in roasting pan (about 3 lbs. meat). Pour on honey. Let stand for one-half hour. Turn ribs over and baste thoroughly with sauce. Let stand another half-hour. Place in 350 degree oven and roast (on rack if crispness is desired) for one hour and twenty minutes. Turn and baste occasionally while cooking. Serves 4.

Spicy Dry Barbecue Mix

Cathy Allen – Capitola, California

1/2 cup mild **Mexican Chile Powder**	1/4 tsp. **Onion Powder**
1/4 tsp. **Curry Powder**	1/4 tsp. **Garlic Powder**
1/4 tsp. **Dry Mustard**	1/4 tsp. **White Pepper**
1/4 tsp. dried **Oregano Leaves**	1/2 tsp. **Celery Salt**
1/4 tsp. dried **Parsley Flakes**	**Peanut Oil**

Crush oregano leaves and parsley flakes finely between fingers. Mix all dry ingredients well together, and put in hand shaker. With a food brush, brush oil over the food to be barbecued. Generously sprinkle barbecue mix over oil, and spread in well with brush or fingers. If continued coating is desired during barbecuing, stir some barbecue mix in with a little oil, and brush on. Barbecue mix should cover about six chickens, steaks, fish, etc.

Dry Poultry Seasoning

Walter Jetton's LBJ Barbecue Cook Book (Courtesy Simon & Schuster)

6 tbsp. **Salt**	2 tbsp. **Ground Bay Leaves**
3 tbsp. **Black Pepper**	1 tbsp. **Paprika**
2 tbsp. **MSG** (or other pep powder)	2 tbsp. **Dry Mustard**
2 tbsp. **Garlic Powder**	

Sprinkle this on chicken and fowl before barbecuing. Makes about one pound of dry seasoning.

Mop for All Barbecue Meats

Walter Jetton's LBJ Barbecue Cook Book (Courtesy Simon & Schuster)

3 tbsp. **Salt**
3 tbsp. **Dry Mustard**
2 tbsp. **Garlic Powder**
1 tbsp. **Ground Bay Leaves**
2 tbsp. **Chili Powder**
3 tbsp. **Paprika**

2 tbsp. **Louisiana Hot Sauce**
2 pints **Worcestershire Sauce**
1 pint **Vinegar**
4 quarts **Beef Bone Stock**
1 pint **Oil**
3 tbsp. **MSG** (or other pep powder)

Use this mop to rub over meats or to baste them while cooking. The flavor will change and improve during use, for you are constantly transferring smoke and grease from the meats back to the mop concoction. Keep leftover mop refrigerated.

To make bone stock, buy stout beef bones and boil them. Add all the other ingredients to bone stock and let stand overnight in refrigerator before using. Makes about 6 quarts of mop.

Merle's Mop Sauce

Merle Ellis – "The Butcher"
(Reprinted by permission of *Chronicle Features*, San Francisco)

1 cup **Vinegar** (cider or wine)
5 tbsp. **Worcestershire Sauce**
2/3 cup **Salad Oil**
3 tbsp. **Butter**

1 **Lemon**, thinly sliced
2 to 3 cloves **Garlic**, minced
3 tbsp. grated **Fresh Ginger**
2 tbsp. **Dry Mustard**

Combine all ingredients in a saucepan and heat until flavors are nicely blended. Use to baste any meat or poultry.

Sauces, Rubs, Mops and Marinades

Recipe:_____

From:_____

Ingredients:

_____   _____

_____   _____

_____   _____

_____   _____

_____   _____

Directions:_____

_____

_____

_____

_____

Recipe:_____

From:_____

Ingredients:

_____   _____

_____   _____

_____   _____

_____   _____

_____   _____

Directions:_____

_____

_____

_____

_____

Beef

Beef

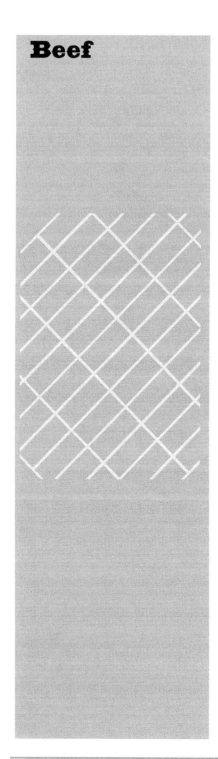

Beef Grilling Guides

(Table courtesy of National Live Stock and Meat Board)

Beef Cuts	Thickness	Temperature of Coals	Open Grill (Direct Heat) Rare to Medium	Covered Cooker Rare to Medium
Ground beef patties				
3 per pound	3/4 inch	medium	12 to 14 min.	10 to 12 min.
	1/2 inch	medium	10 to 12 min.	8 to 10 min.
4 per pound	1/2 inch	medium	10 to 12 min.	8 to 10 min.
Chuck steak*	3/4 to 1 inch	medium	14 to 20 min.	10 to 14 min.
	1 1/2 inches	medium-low	18 to 24 min.	14 to 20 min.
Rib steak, Rib eye steak	3/4 inch	medium	12 to 15 min.	8 to 12 min.
Top loin steak	1 inch	medium	15 to 20 min.	10 to 14 min.
	1 1/2 inches	medium-low	25 to 30 min.	16 to 20 min.
Sirloin steak,	3/4 inch	medium	12 to 16 min.	10 to 14 min.
Porterhouse steak,	1 inch	medium	16 to 20 min.	14 to 18 min.
T-bone steak,	1 1/2 inches	medium-low	22 to 30 min.	20 to 24 min.
Top sirloin steak				
Top round steak*	3/4 to 1 inch	medium	22 to 26 min.	20 to 24 min.
	1 1/2 inches	medium-low	28 to 35 min.	26 to 30 min.
Tenderloin		medium-high	30 to 45 min.	30 to 45 min.
(whole, 4 to 6 pounds)				
Tenderloin steaks	1 inch	medium	6 to 8 min.	5 to 7 min.
	1 1/2 inches	medium	8 to 10 min.	7 to 9 min.
	2 inches	medium-low	10 to 12 min.	8 to 10 min.
Flank steak		medium	12 to 15 min.	10 to 12 min.

Beef Grilling Guides

(Table courtesy of National Live Stock and Meat Board)

Beef Roasts	Weight	Temperature of Coals	Covered Cooker (Indirect Heat) minutes per lb.	Rotisserie (Indirect Heat) minutes per lb.
Boneless chuck*	3 to 4 pounds	medium-low	25 to 30 min.	30 to 35 min.
Boneless rump*	4 to 6 pounds	medium-low	20 to 25 min.	25 to 30 min.
Boneless top round*	4 to 6 pounds	medium-low	15 to 20 min.	22 to 27 min.
Rib eye	4 to 6 pounds	medium-low	15 to 20 min.	18 to 24 min.
Round Tip*	5 to 8 pounds	medium-low	20 to 25 min.	25 to 30 min.
	3 to 5 pounds	medium-low	25 to 30 min.	30 to 35 min.

*High quality

Note: Gas grills (natural gas or LP), consult owner's manual for cooking instructions. The timetable is based upon the surface of the beef being four to five inches from the coals.

Barbecued Chuck Roast

Weston W. Ross – La Puente, California

3 to 4 lb. **Round** or **7-bone Chuck Roast** (cut two inches thick)
1 1/2 to 2 tsp. **Meat Tenderizer**
2 to 3 **Green Onions**, chopped
1 large clove **Garlic**
1/4 diced **Green Pepper**
2 stalks **Celery**, diced
1/2 tsp. **Dried Oregano**
1/2 tsp. **Dried Rosemary**
Dash **Cayenne**
1 tbsp. **Worcestershire Sauce**
3/4 cup **Burgundy Wine**
3 tbsp. **Peanut Oil**

Slash fat edges. Sprinkle both sides of roast evenly with meat tenderizer. Pierce meat deeply all over with fork.

Place in shallow dish and top with green onions, garlic, green pepper, celery, oregano, rosemary and cayenne.

Combine Worcestershire, burgundy and oil and pour over meat. Refrigerate overnight, turning meat several times, each time spooning the chopped ingredients over top again.

Sear both sides over glowing coals. Raise grill and continue cooking, having meat about six inches from heat, until done as desired. Allow from 50 to 60 minutes for total cooking time. Brush frequently during cooking with any remaining marinade. Makes 4 to 6 servings.

Tip: To sear the surface of a cut of meat, lower the grill rack two to three inches above coals for the first two to three minutes of cooking time. Sear once on each side. Then raise rack immediately.

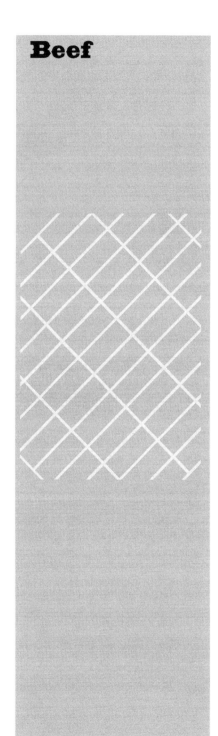

Beef

Barbecued Beef

Agri-Business Council – Phoenix, Arizona

1 whole **Beef Brisket**

Place on broiling pan so grease will cook off. Cover with foil and bake at 325 degrees for about five hours (or until extremely tender). Let cool. Shred or cut into very small pieces. Add to Barbecue Sauce in crockery slow cooker and simmer for two hours. Serves 20.

Aunt Polly's Barbecue Sauce

Courtesy Susan Nunn, Tempe, Arizona

1 can (28 oz.) **Tomatoes**
2 large **Onions**, chopped
5 oz. **Worcestershire Sauce**
1 can (15 1/2 oz.) **Crushed Pineapple**, drained
1/2 cup (or more) **Molasses** or **Honey** to taste
Fresh **Ground Pepper** to taste
1 bottle (28 oz.) **Hickory-flavored Barbecue Sauce**

In crockery slow cooker, combine ingredients, (except for Barbecue Sauce) breaking up canned tomatoes with a spoon. Add bottled barbecue sauce and simmer for about five hours.

Death Row Barbecue Brisket

R. Gordon Root – Burke, Virginia

1 can (12 oz.) **Pineapple Juice**
6 oz. **Apple Juice**
4 to 6 lbs. first cut **Beef Brisket**
3 tbsp. **Butter**
2 large **Onions**, finely chopped
4 cloves **Garlic**, minced
1 bottle (44 oz.) **Ketchup**
1/4 cup **Molasses**
2 tbsp. **Mustard**

2 tbsp. **Worcestershire Sauce**
1 tbsp. **Soy Sauce**
2 tbsp. **Mexican Oregano**
20 to 30 drops **Tabasco®**
   Pepper Sauce
1 tsp. **Salt**
1 tbsp. **Lemon Juice**
1 can (12 oz.) **Beer** (use to thin)
2 tbsp. **Frozen Orange Juice**

Marinade meat from six to ten hours in pineapple and apple juices. Cook onions and garlic in butter until transparent. Add the balance of sauce ingredients and heat but do not cook. Smoke meat in a heat type smoker (charcoal type). Place remaining marinade in water pan in smoker. Place meat on top rack and close smoker.

Soak wood chunks (mesquite, apple or hickory) in water half an hour and place on charcoal to create smoke. Smoke/cook four to six hours, depending on smoker efficiency. Baste with barbecue sauce after smoke has disappeared. (Note: every time cooker is lifted, additional cooking time of half an hour will be required.) Recipe serves 15 to 20.

Tip: Before barbecuing, slash through fat on the outside of steaks at one-inch intervals to prevent curling.

Spicy Barbecued Steak

Barbecue Industry Association

3 lb. **Chuck Blade Steak**
(cut 1" thick, trimmed)
1 1/2 tsp. **Adolph's® 100% Natural Meat Tenderizer-Seasoned**
1 cup **Ketchup**
1/2 cup **Water**

1/4 cup **Soy Sauce**
2 tbsp. **Vinegar**
1 tbsp. **Brown Sugar**
1 tsp. **Mustard**
1 tsp. **Horseradish**
1 clove **Garlic**, crushed

In small saucepan, combine ketchup, water, soy sauce, vinegar, brown sugar, mustard, horseradish and garlic. Simmer for 10 to 15 minutes on back of grill.

Moisten steak with water. Sprinkle evenly with half the tenderizer and pierce deeply with a fork. Repeat on other side. (Use no salt.) Grill steak five inches from medium-hot coals about 35 minutes, turning and basting frequently with sauce. Serves 6.

Juicy Burgers

By Permission: Lea & Perrins, Inc.

1 lb. **Ground Beef**
2 tbsp. chopped **Onion**
1/4 cup **Lea & Perrins® Steak Sauce**, divided

In a medium bowl, combine beef, onion and two tablespoons of the Lea & Perrins® Steak Sauce. Shape into four 3 1/2-inch patties. Cook on a grill over hot coals. Makes 4 burgers.

Tip: Keep a bottle of water with a sprayer top near the grill to douse unexpected flame flare-ups.

Carne Asada

Courtesy National Livestock and Meat Board

4 well-trimmed **Beef Rib Eye Steaks** (cut 3/4-inch thick)
2 tbsp. fresh **Lime Juice**
6 **Flour Tortillas** (6-inch diameter)
1/4 cup each shredded **Colby** and **Monterey Jack Cheese**
Salsa

Place steaks in a utility dish. Sprinkle with half the lime juice, rubbing into surface. Turn steaks and repeat using remaining lime juice. Cover and refrigerate while preparing coals.

Wrap tortillas securely in heavy-duty aluminum foil.

Place steaks on grid over medium coals. Grill steaks for 12 to 15 minutes for rare (140 degrees) to medium (160 degrees) or to desired doneness, turning once.

Five minutes before end of cooking time, place tortilla packet on outer edge of grid. Heat tortillas five minutes, turning packet once.

Top each steak with an equal amount of cheese. Serve with salsa and tortillas. (Steaks will yield three cooked, trimmed servings per pound)

Salsa

2 medium **Tomatoes**, seeded and coarsely chopped
2 tbsp. thinly sliced **Green Onion**
3 tsp. chopped **Cilantro** or **Parsley**
3 tsp. **Red Wine Vinegar**
2 small cloves **Garlic**, minced
1/4 tsp. each **Salt** and **Coarse Ground Black Pepper**
1 to 2 **Jalapeno Peppers**, seeded and minced

Combine all ingredients and use for steak topping.

Tip: Cooking times will vary, depending on the type of grill, the climate, and the distance of food from the heat.

Helen's Barbecue Sauce

Helen Fraczkowski – Lorain, Ohio

1 **Onion**, chopped
2 tbsp. **Oil**
2 tbsp. **Vinegar**
2 tbsp. **Brown Sugar**
4 tbsp. **Lemon Juice**

1 cup **Ketchup**
3 tbsp. **Worcestershire Sauce**
1/2 cup **Water**
Salt

Brown onion in fat and add remaining ingredients. Simmer for thirty minutes. Makes two cups.

Best Barbecued Meatballs

Beverly Luck – Ward, Arkansas

Mix together:

1 1/2 lbs. **Ground Beef**
1/2 cup **Milk**

2 tsp. **Salt**
1/4 tsp. **Pepper**

Shape into balls and brown in small amount of fat. Combine:

1 cup **Ketchup**
1/4 cup **Worcestershire Sauce**
1 tsp. **Sugar**

2 tbsp. **Vinegar**
3 tbsp. chopped **Onion**
1 tbsp. **Water**

and pour over meat in skillet. Cover and cook slowly ten minutes, turning occasionally. Makes 16 meatballs.

Tip: If using a gas grill, clean or replace the briquettes frequently to prevent flare-ups from briquettes soaked with grease.

Bar-B-Q Beef

Jean Emanuel – Yuma, Arizona

6 lbs. **Lean Beef Roast**
1 tbsp. **Liquid Smoke**
2 bottles (10 or 12 oz.)
    Bar-B-Q Sauce
1/2 cup **Water**
2 tbsp. **Onion Flakes**

1 cup **Ketchup**
1 tsp. **Liquid Smoke**
1 tbsp. **Mustard**
1 tsp. **Garlic Salt**
2 tbsp. **Sugar**
Dash **Worcestershire Sauce**

Sprinkle roast with liquid smoke and let stand for 20 minutes. Sear on top of stove in roaster or in Dutch oven, and then either pop in oven or cover Dutch oven and bake at about 300 degrees for 20 minutes. Remove from oven and add 1/2 bottle Bar-B-Q Sauce, water and onion flakes.

Return to oven for three hours (or until meat is tender). Remove meat from pan and shred, slice or cube. Add to sauce in roaster the remaining bottled Bar-B-Q sauce and all other ingredients. Return meat to sauce and simmer for about 20 minutes. Serve over opened hamburger buns or rice. Serves 8-10.

Marinated BBQ Chuck Steak

Gloria Huggins – Madison, Florida

1/3 cup **Olive Oil**
1 tbsp. **Chili Powder**
2 tsp. **Ginger**
1 tsp. **Salt**

2 tbsp. minced **Onion**
1/4 cup **Lemon Juice**
2-3 lb. **Chuck Steak**

Combine all ingredients EXCEPT steak for marinade. Pour over steak, coating both sides with marinade. Place steak on grill, cooking 8 to 10 minutes each side (or until desired degree of doneness).

Texas Beef Barbecue

Walter Jetton's LBJ Barbecue Cook Book
(Courtesy Simon & Schuster)

3 **Bay Leaves**
1 cup **Water**
2 quarts **Bone Stock**

Salt and **Pepper**
6 lbs. **Beef Brisket**

Put bay leaves into a cup of water and bring to a boil. Let water simmer 10 minutes, then remove leaves and add bay tea to bone stock, along with salt and pepper. Put brisket in Dutch oven and add stock mixture to cover it about a quarter of the way. Cover and cook over fire, turning brisket about every half hour until it's nearly done. (Test for doneness by forking.) Mop brisket and lay it on the grill to finish cooking, being sure to turn it and to mop it every 20 minutes or so.

To make a natural gravy, add a little **Worcestershire Sauce** and dash of **Chili Powder** to liquid in which brisket was cooked.

Marinated London Broil

By Permission: Lea & Perrins, Inc.

1 1/2 lbs. **Flank Steak** (Or round or shoulder)
1/2 cup **Lea & Perrins® Steak Sauce**
4 tsp. **Lemon Juice**
2 tsp. **Lea & Perrins® Worcestershire Sauce**
1/4 tsp. **Salt**

Place steak in a shallow glass pan. Prick with fork tines on both sides.

To prepare marinade: Combine Lea & Perrins® Steak Sauce, lemon juice, Lea & Perrins® Worcestershire Sauce and salt. Pour over steak, coating both sides. Marinate for one hour.

To cook over charcoal: place steak on a rack over hot coals until done as desired (10 to 15 minutes for medium), turning and brushing often with marinade. Serves 4 to 6.

✑Tip: To have a successful fire in a grill, use enough charcoal briquettes to cover the actual grilling area. Stack the briquettes in pyramid fashion so they will light faster (since air can circulate around them).

Flank Steak BBQ

Ann H. Martin – Flagstaff, Arizona

2 **Flank Steaks** (1 1/2 lbs. each)
1 cup **Chili Sauce**
1/2 cup **Red Wine Vinegar**
1 cup **Red Wine**
2 tbsp. **Worcestershire Sauce**
1/2 tsp **Onion Powder**
1/4 tsp **Garlic Powder**

2 tsp. **Mustard**
1 tsp. **Salt**
1/4 cup **Salad Oil**
1 can **Consommé**
3 tbsp. **Cornstarch**
 (dissolved in 3 tbsp. water)

Combine ingredients for marinade. Let steaks stand in marinade in refrigerator for three to twelve hours. Drain meat one half hour before grilling, and save marinade. Add consommé and cornstarch to marinade and heat to boiling. Brush steaks with heated marinade. Broil steaks three to four inches from coals for about 12 minutes per side. Cut across grain in narrow strips. Serves 6.

Grilled Chuck Roast

Greer Neal – Scottsdale, Arizona

5 to 6 lb. **Roast** (chuck, rib, etc. A blade chuck roast cut 3 inch thick is fine)
1 bottle (5 oz.) **Soy Sauce**
1 tbsp. **Worcestershire Sauce**
Juice of 1 **Lemon**

1/4 cup **Brown Sugar**
1/2 cup **Bourbon**
1 1/2 cups **Water**

Marinate roast overnight in refrigerator, turning once or twice. Drain meat. Broil over very low coals on a charcoal grill for one hour, turning every 15 minutes, brushing with marinade each time. (Roast will be rare with one hour of cooking.)

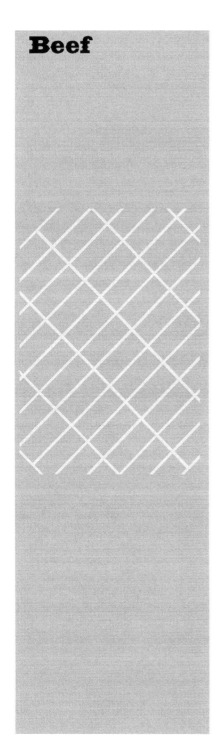

Taichung Steaks

Li-Chen Hillhouse – Live Oak, Florida

2 lbs. of **T-Bone Steaks**
1/4 tsp. **Adolph's Meat Tenderizer**
1 tsp. **Salad Oil**
2 tsp. **Worcestershire Sauce**
1 tsp. **Brown Sugar**

1/2 cup **Ketchup** or **Tomato Paste**
4 or 5 drops **Tabasco® Pepper Sauce**
Dash **Garlic Salt**

Start the charcoal and wait until it is burning evenly. Place grill approximately six inches above the level of the charcoal.

Sprinkle tenderizer on steaks and pound in well with tenderizing mallet or back of cleaver. Place steaks on grill and brown both sides evenly. Mix remaining ingredients in a bowl and brush on steaks as they finish cooking. To get uniformly cooked meat, steaks should be turned every 10 to 15 minutes, and take at least an hour to cook a half-inch steak. Serves 4 to 6.

Old Tucson Barbecue Beef

Courtesy: Old Tucson

5 lbs. **Top Round Roast** (pre-cooked to medium rare, cut in slices)

Apply **Old Tucson Barbecue Sauce** (next page) in between slices of meat and pour remainder of sauce over slices. Heat in 350 degree oven for approximately 30 minutes. Makes double servings for 12.

Old Tucson Barbecue Sauce

Courtesy Old Tucson Corporation

1/4 cup **Lemon Juice**
1/3 cup **Chile Sauce** or **Ketchup**
1 tsp. prepared **Horseradish**
1 tsp. **Worcestershire Sauce**
1/2 tsp. each **Salt** and **Paprika**

1/2 cup **Orange Juice**
2 tsp. **Dry Mustard**
1/4 cup firmly packed **Brown Sugar**
1 clove **Garlic**, minced or mashed
2 **Lemons**, sliced

Combine all ingredients (except meat). Apply sauce in between slices of meat and pour remainder of sauce over slices. Heat in 350 degree oven for approximately 30 minutes.

Oven Barbecued Brisket

Millie Boyd – Edgewood, Maryland

7-9 lb. **Brisket of Beef**
Instant Meat Tenderizer
1 1/2 cups **Hickory Flavored Barbecue Sauce**
1 1/2 tbsp. **Worcestershire Sauce**

1 tbsp. minced **Onion**
1 tsp. **Liquid Smoke**
1 tsp. **Garlic Salt**
1/2 tsp. **Pepper**

Trim away excess fat from meat. Pierce both sides of brisket with fork and sprinkle moderately with tenderizer. Place in roasting pan large enough to lay meat flat. Blend remaining ingredients and pour over meat. Cover and refrigerate six hours (or overnight). Cover with foil and bake at 300 degrees for 4 1/2 to 5 1/2 hours. Slice across the grain. Serves 10.

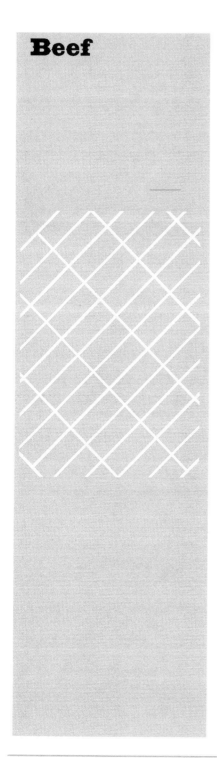

Beef

Down South Barbecue

Wanda M. Smith – Drakes Branch, Va.

4 to 5 lbs. **Beef Roast** (or pork roast)
Salt and **Pepper** to taste
2 **Onions**, sliced

2 cups **Water**
1 bottle (16 oz.) **Barbecue Sauce**
1 large **Onion**, chopped

Salt and pepper meat. Put one-half of sliced onion in bottom of crock pot, then add meat and water. Add remainder of sliced onion on top of meat. Cover and cook overnight. Remove bone and fat from meat when done (or when meat pulls away easily from bone).

Put meat back in crock pot. Add barbecue sauce and chopped onion. Cover and cook additional three to five hours on high or eight to twelve hours on low. Stir two or three times during cooking. Makes at least eight sandwiches.

Chicken

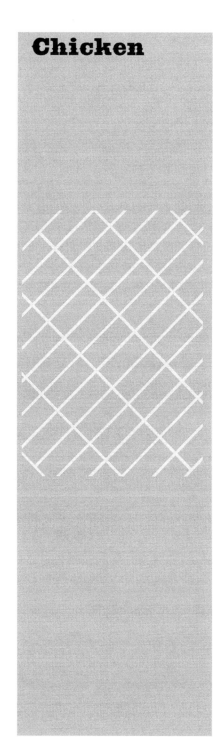

Chicken

Teri-Mesquite Chicken

Desert Mesquite of Arizona – Phoenix, AZ.

Preparation of Grill

4 to 6 ozs. **Arizona Mesquite Wood Barbecue Chips**

Soak wood chips in water approximately one half-hour prior to using. Light barbecue grill so it is ready for cooking approximately one half-hour before serving time. (Gas or electric grills should be set on "low." A charcoal fire should be "cool"). When grill is ready, sprinkle wood chips on coal or volcanic rock.

Marinade

2 lbs. boned **Chicken**
4 tsp. **Honey**
1/3 cup **Dry White Wine**

1 tbsp. **Olive Oil**
1 clove **Garlic**, chopped
1/2 tsp. grated **Fresh Ginger**

Combine honey, wine, oil, garlic and ginger in a shallow dish (approximately 10×10). Blend lightly with a fork. Place chicken in marinade, coating all over. Marinate in refrigerator for two hours, turning chicken every half hour.

Broil chicken on grill, taking care not to burn marinade. (If grill has a cover, use it to capture the mesquite wood smoke.) The chicken will take about half an hour to cook, depending on how hot grill is.

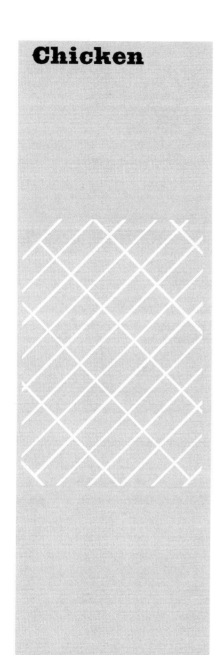

Joan's Oriental BBQ Chicken

Joan Cordiero – Davidsonville, Maryland

1 **Fryer** (cut up)
2 cups **Wine**
1 tsp. **Ground Ginger**
1 cup **Grapefruit Juice**

2 cups **Soy Sauce**
Garlic Powder to taste
2 **Green Onions**, sliced very
thin, including tops

Mix all ingredients (EXCEPT chicken) and simmer for 20 minutes. Put chicken parts in marinade, cover and store overnight in refrigerator (or at least six hours), turning occasionally. Barbecue parts on grill, using marinade to baste.

Home Barbecued Chicken

Linda Rivel – Lancaster, Pa.

2 **Broilers**
1/3 cup **Cider Vinegar**
1 tsp. **Kitchen Bouquet**
1 tsp. **Worcestershire Sauce**
1/2 tsp. **Onion Salt**
1/4 tsp. **Garlic Salt**

1/2 tsp. **Salt**
1/8 tsp. **Pepper**
1 tbsp. **Tomato Paste**
1/2 cup melted **Butter**
Dash **Paprika**

Make a sauce of ingredients (EXCEPT broilers) and set aside. Split broilers down the back. Wash and clean thoroughly, then wipe dry. Grease a broiling pan and rack, and heat. When hot, place chickens on rack under a very hot flame. Sear both sides, turning frequently. Reduce oven heat to 400 degrees and finish broiling. Use sauce to baste chickens several times during broiling.

Oven Barbecued Chicken

Mrs. Robert Perry – Fredricksburg, Virginia

2 1/2 to 3 lbs. **Chicken**
(cut up, or equivalent in parts)
1 cup **Ketchup**
1/4 cup **Worcestershire Sauce**
1/4 cup **Soy Sauce**
1/2 tsp. **Thyme**
1/4 tsp. **Garlic Powder**

1 medium **Onion**, chopped fine
1/4 cup **Vinegar**
1/4 cup lightly packed **Brown Sugar**
1/2 tsp. **Salt**
1/4 tsp. **Black Pepper**
1/2 stick **Butter** or **Margarine** melted

Make sauce by mixing all ingredients (EXCEPT chicken). Place chicken parts in single layer in baking pan, skin side up. Pour sauce over chicken and bake in 350 degree oven, uncovered, about one hour (or until chicken is done). Serves 8.

Lemon Barbeque Chicken

Mrs. James K. Griffin – Patterson, Georgia

2 **Broilers** (2 1/2 to 3 lbs.)
1 cup **Salad Oil**
1/2 cup fresh **Lemon Juice**
1 1/2 tbsp. **Salt**
1 1/2 tsp. **Paprika**

2 tsp. **Crushed Basil**
1/2 tsp. **Garlic Powder**
2 tsp. **Onion Powder**
1/2 tsp. **Crushed Thyme**

Split chicken in halves or quarters. Place in shallow baking pan. Combine all other ingredients in a jar and shake well to blend. Pour sauce over chicken. Cover tightly and marinate in refrigerator from six to eight hours (or overnight), turning chicken pieces occasionally. Remove chicken from refrigerator about one-half before grilling. Place chicken on grill, skin side up, and grill 20 minutes, brushing often with sauce. Turn chicken and grill additional 20 minutes. Serves 4 to 6.

Grilled Chicken and Sausages

Barbecue Industry Association

1/2 cup **Butter** or **Margarine**	1/8 tsp. **Cinnamon**
1 medium clove **Garlic**, crushed	1/8 tsp. crushed **Tarragon**
3/4 tsp. **Salt**	1 **Broiler-Fryer Chicken** (3 lbs.)
3/4 tsp. crushed **Summer Savory**	cut up
1/2 tsp. **Paprika**	1 lb. sweet **Italian Pork Sausages**

Melt butter. Stir in garlic clove, salt, savory, paprika, cinnamon and tarragon.

Place chicken and sausages on grill. Brush with butter mixture. Grill about four inches from medium hot coals until chicken is tender (about 30 to 40 minutes), basting and turning chicken and sausages occasionally. Makes 6 servings.

Korean-Style Chicken

Courtesy Best Foods – New Jersey

1/4 cup **Sesame Seeds**	1 clove **Garlic**, crushed
1/4 cup **Corn Oil**	1/4 tsp. **Pepper**
1/4 cup **Soy Sauce**	1/4 tsp. **Ginger**
1/4 cup **Karo® Dark Corn Syrup**	1 **Broiler-Fryer Chicken**
1 small **Onion**, sliced	(cut into pieces)

In a shallow baking dish stir together the first eight ingredients. Add chicken, turning to coat. Cover and refrigerate, turning once, at least three hours.

Grill over low coals, turning and basting frequently, about 50 minutes. Makes 4 servings.

Tip: Always start cooking chicken parts by placing cut side toward heat to seal in juices.

Orange Barbecued Chicken

By Permission: Lea & Perrins®, Inc.

1/2 cup **Lea & Perrins® Steak Sauce**
1/4 cup **Orange Juice**
3/4 tsp. grated **Orange Peel** (optional)

1/4 tsp. **Ginger**
3 lbs. **Chicken Parts**

To prepare marinade combine Lea & Perrins® Steak Sauce, orange juice, orange peel and ginger; set aside. Place chicken in a baking pan. Pierce all sides with fork tines. Coat completely with marinade. Let stand for 15 minutes.

To grill over charcoal: place chicken on a rack over slow burning coals. Cook until juices run clear when pierced with a knife (about 45 minutes), turning often and brushing occasionally with marinade.

To bake: place chicken in a single layer, skin side up in a shallow baking pan. Bake in a preheated 350 degree oven until juices run clear when pierced with a knife (about one hour), turning often and brushing occasionally with marinade. Yield: 4 portions, 3/4 cup sauce.

Tip: To LOWER the temperature of a charcoal briquette fire, RAISE the grid or spread out the coals.

To RAISE the temperature, tap the ash from the coals or push the coals closer.

Very Tasty Bar-be-Qued Chicken

Beth Gaddy – Chapel Hill, North Carolina

2 to 3 lb. **Chicken** (cut up)   3/4 stick **Butter**
1 cup **Coca Cola®**   **Salt** and **Pepper** to taste
1 cup **Ketchup**

Mix together Coca Cola® and ketchup until well blended. Place chicken in a large baking dish; add salt and pepper to taste. Dot pats of butter on each piece of chicken. Pour ketchup mixture over chicken and bake in 350 degree oven, uncovered, for one to one and one-half hours (depending on degree of brown desired).

Spiced Chicken B-B-Q

Charlotte Farmer – Richmond, Virginia

2 tbsp. **Cooking Oil**   2 tsp. **Brown Sugar**
1/4 cup chopped fine **Onion**   1 tsp. **Celery Seed**
1 clove **Garlic**, minced   1 tsp. **Dry Mustard**
3/4 cup **Ketchup**   1/2 tsp. **Salt**
1/3 cup **Vinegar**   1/4 tsp. **Black Pepper**
1 tbsp. **Worcestershire Sauce**   1/4 tsp. **Hot Pepper Sauce**
                                     2 1/2 to 3 lbs. **Chicken** (quartered)

Heat cooking oil in saucepan and cook onion and garlic until tender, but do not brown. Add ketchup, stir, and add remaining ingredients (EXCEPT chicken). Bring to a boil. Reduce heat, simmer, uncovered, for 10 minutes, stirring occasionally. Set sauce aside.

Season chicken pieces with additional salt, if desired. Place chicken pieces bone side down over medium to hot coals. Grill 25 minutes (until bone side is well browned). Turn pieces over and grill 25 minutes more (until chicken is tender). Brush chicken frequently with sauce during last 10 minutes of grilling, using all the sauce.

Tip: Chicken requires turning every five to eight minutes to prevent skin from blistering and loss of juices. To turn, USE TONGS, not forks.

Grannie Morris' Barbecued Chicken

Helen G. Morris – Prescott, Arkansas

3 lb. **Frying Chicken**
Flour (for dredging)
Salt and **Pepper**
1/2 cup **Cooking Oil**
1 can (6 oz.) **Tomato Sauce**
4 **Green Onions**, chopped fine
3 cloves **Garlic**, chopped fine

1 tbsp. **Barbecue Spices**
3/4 tsp. **Chile Powder**
1/4 tsp. **Basil**
1/4 tsp. **Celery Salt**
1 1/3 cups **Water**
2 tbsp. **Worcestershire Sauce**
Dash **Tabasco® Pepper Sauce**

Dredge chicken pieces in flour, salt and pepper. Brown in one-half inch hot oil. Combine remaining ingredients in a bowl. Place browned chicken pieces in casserole and pour barbecue sauce over them. Cover and bake in 350 degree oven one hour (or until chicken is tender). For crispy crust, remove cover during last half hour of cooking.

Italian B-B-Q Chicken

Charlotte Farmer – Richmond, Virginia

8 pieces of **Chicken**
1/2 cup **Vinegar**
1/4 cup **Lemon Juice**

1 stick **Butter** or **Margarine**
1 tsp. **Morton Natural Seasoning**
1/4 cup **Italian Dressing**

Combine all ingredients (EXCEPT chicken). Heat in saucepan until butter is melted. Pour over chicken parts. Marinade (covered) at least two hours in refrigerator. Place chicken parts on outdoor grill and cook slowly for about one hour. Turn frequently, basting with remaining sauce.

Oven Bar-B-Que for Chicken Parts

Mrs. Brenda Glover – Tehuacana, Texas

1 **Chicken Fryer** (cut into parts)

Dry Ingredients

2 cups **Flour**

1/4 tsp. **Garlic Powder**

1/4 tsp. **Celery Salt**

1/4 tsp. **Oregano**

1/4 tsp. **Black Pepper**

1/2 tsp. **Chili Powder**

1 tsp. **Salt**

Put all dry ingredients into a sifter and sift into a quart-size bowl.

Wet Ingredients

1/4 cup **Liquid Smoke**

1/4 cup **Ketchup**

1 **Egg**

In another quart-size bowl put wet ingredients. Mix well. Cut up one chicken fryer and dip parts first in wet bowl mix, then dry mix. Using a cookie sheet with edge, coat well with one-quarter cup cooking oil. Place coated fryer parts on cookie sheet, skin side down, and bake for 30 minutes at 350 degrees. Turn over and bake for another 20 minutes (or until well done).

Tip: Grill chicken over a medium-high bed of coals, about four to six inches above coals.

Tropical Chicken

Barbecue Industry Association

1/3 cup **Pineapple Juice**
1 tbsp. **Vegetable Oil**
1 tsp. **Salt**
1 tsp. **Ginger**
1/2 tsp. dried **Thyme Leaves**

1/4 tsp. **Ground Turmeric**
1/4 tsp. crushed **Hot Red Pepper Flakes**
6 **Chicken Breast Halves** (boned and skinned—about 1 1/2 lbs.)

Prepare a medium-hot charcoal fire. Combine all ingredients (EXCEPT chicken breasts) in a large non-aluminum pan and whisk until well blended.

Rinse chicken with cold water and pat dry. Marinate at room temperature, turning several times to coat well. Remove chicken breasts from marinade and place skinned-side down on an oiled cooking grid set four to six inches above ashed coals.

Grill, turning once and basting occasionally with marinade, until chicken is white throughout but still juicy inside, about eight to ten minutes. Serves 6.

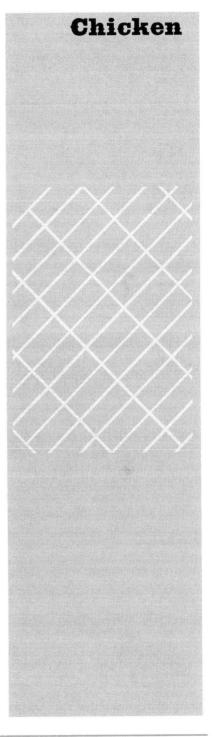

Chicken

Recipe:_____

From:_____

Ingredients:

_____ _____

_____ _____

_____ _____

_____ _____

_____ _____

Directions:_____

_____

_____

_____

_____

Recipe:_____

From:_____

Ingredients:

_____ _____

_____ _____

_____ _____

_____ _____

Directions:_____

_____

_____

_____

_____

Pork

Pork

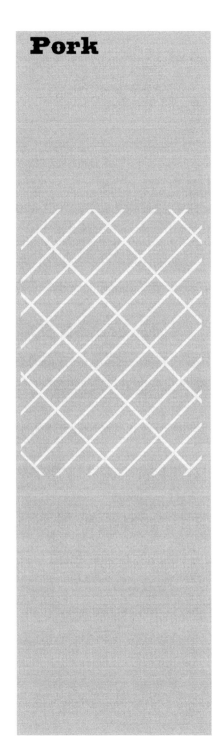

Guide to Cooking the Whole Hog

(Table courtesy North Carolina Pork Producers Council)

1. Select your menu
2. Select a method of preparation; for whole hog or shoulders, etc. using wood, charcoal, or gas

Methods for Cooking*

Weight of Pig	Charcoal	Amount of Gas	Wood	Cooker Temperature	Approximate Cooking Time with Closed Lid
75 lbs.	60 lbs.	40 lb.	1/3 Cord	225°-250°	6 to 7 hours
100 lbs.	70 lbs.	Cylinder	1/3-1/2 Cord	225°-250°	7 to 8 hours
125 lbs.	80 lbs.		1/2 Cord	225°-250°	8 to 9 hours

* **ImPorkant:**
  - DO NOT EXCEED 225° cooking temperature for first 2 hours of cooking.
  - If using an "open" grill allow 1 hour per 10 pounds of pork.
  - Internal temperature of 170° must be reached.
  - When using charcoal or wood distribute more coals under the hams and shoulders and less in the center for more uniform cooking. Additional coals started outside of cooker should be added as needed to maintain proper temperature.
  - If using gas cooker, read manufacturers instructions.

3. **Determine number you plan to serve; allowing 1 1/2 lbs. of carcass weight per person.**
   This will tell you the amount of pork needed to purchase plus estimated cooking time.

A Guideline for Purchasing

75 lbs. dressed pig = approximately 30 lbs. cooked, chopped pork
100 lbs. dressed pig = approximately 40 lbs. cooked, chopped pork
125 lbs. dressed pig = approximately 50 lbs. cooked, chopped pork
14 lbs. uncooked Shoulder = 10 lbs. cooked 6-7 hours
6-7 lbs. uncooked Boston Butt = 3 lbs. cooked 3 1/2 -4 hours
14 lbs. uncooked Ham = 6-7 lbs. cooked 6-7 hours

4. **Where to purchase:**
   - At a State inspected establishment (7 days notice for a local super market, or grocery store, or meat packer is often needed.)

5. **Basic Equipment needed:**
   - Large container such as ice chest, suitable for keeping a temperature of 35° or less up to 24 hours prior to cooking.
   - Large grill surface suitable for method of cooking – wood, charcoal, or gas.
   - Meat thermometer to insure 170° internal temperature for optimum tenderness.

Western Kentucky Pork Barbecue

Deni Hamilton – Louisville, Kentucky

1 fresh Pork Shoulder (9 or 10 pounds)

Pour barbecue sauce over shoulder and put shoulder on a rack on a roasting pan in a cold oven. Turn heat to 200 degrees and roast until it falls apart, about 18 to 20 hours.

Or, roast very slowly over a hickory fire until very tender. Brush roast with sauce two or three times while it's roasting.

When very tender, let it cool enough so meat can be handled without burning you. Tear meat into shreds. Mix with just enough warmed barbeque sauce to moisten it (if desired). This makes about five pounds cooked meat, or enough for about 30 full-sized sandwiches.

Sauce

3 1/2 cups **Water**
1 cup **Ketchup**
3/4 cup **Worcestershire Sauce**
2 tsp. **Paprika**
1 1/2 tsp. **Black Pepper**
1 1/2 tsp. **Garlic Salt**

1 1/2 tsp. **Cayenne Pepper**
2 tsp. **Dry Mustard**
5 tsp. **Onion Powder**
3 tbsp. **Salt**

Mix all ingredients and boil for five minutes, stirring frequently. Makes about one quart sauce.

Tip: Wash hands thoroughly with hot soapy water before and after handling pork products.

Savory Grilled Pork Steaks

National Pork Producers Council

3 **Pork Blade Steaks** (cut 1/2 to 3/4 inch thick)
1 tbsp. **Brown Sugar**
1 to 2 tsp. **Curry Powder**
1/4 cup **Soy Sauce**
1 can (8 oz.) **Tomato Sauce**
1 small **Onion,** chopped

Combine brown sugar and curry powder in a small saucepan and mix well. Gradually add soy sauce, tomato sauce and onion, stirring to combine. Bring to a boil, reduce heat and cook slowly five minutes. Cool mixture. Place steaks in plastic bag or baking dish. Add marinade, turning steaks to coat. Tie bag securely or cover dish and marinate in refrigerator four hours or overnight. Drain, reserving marinade. Place steaks on grill over low to medium coals. Cook 30 to 40 minutes or until done, brushing with marinade and turning occasionally. Serves 4.

Lime-Glazed Pork Chops

Courtesy Best Foods – New Jersey

1/3 cup **Karo® Dark Corn Syrup**
1/2 cup grated **Lime Rind**
1/3 cup **Lime Juice**
1 tbsp. **Soy Sauce**
1/4 tsp. **Cloves**
6 **Pork Chops** (1 inch thick)

In a small bowl stir together the first five ingredients. Grill chops six inches from heat, turning once, for 30 minutes. Baste with lime mixture. Grill 30 minutes longer, turning and basting frequently, until chops are tender and glazed. Serves 4.

Tip: Always marinate pork in the refrigerator— never at room temperature.

Sweet and Sour Pork Loin

National Pork Producers Council

4 to 5 lb. boneless **Pork Loin Roast**
(double loin, rolled, and tied)
1 cup packed **Brown Sugar**
3/4 cup **Teriyaki Sauce**
3/4 cup **Dry Red Wine**

3/4 cup **Chili Sauce**
1/2 tsp. **Cloves**
1/4 tsp. **Pepper**
1/8 tsp. **Garlic Powder**

For marinade, combine sugar, sauces, wine, cloves, pepper and powder and mix well. Place roast in a plastic bag and set in shallow baking dish. Pour marinade over roast. Close bag and tie securely. Marinate in refrigerator eight hours (or overnight), turning roast occasionally.

Make a foil drip pan about one and one-half inches deep, extending three inches beyond each side of meat. Position drip pan under meat. Drain roast, reserving marinade. Place roast on grill over low coals. Insert meat thermometer in thickest part of roast, not touching fat or rotisserie rod. Close grill hood. Grill two to two and one-half hours (or until meat thermometer registers 165 degrees). Brush frequently with marinade during last 45 minutes of grilling.

Let roast stand 10 to 15 minutes before carving to allow juices to set and internal temperature to rise to 170 degrees. Serves 10 to 12.

Tip: If marinade is used as a sauce with pork, heat marinade to boiling and boil at least one minute before using. Discard any leftover marinade—do not use again!

Marinated Pork Tenderloin Birds

Steven R. Sutter – Bluffton, Ohio

Marinade

1 tbsp. **Lemon Juice**
1/2 clove **Garlic**
1 tsp. **Cinnamon**
1 tsp. **Salt**
1/4 tsp. **Ginger**

1 cup **Chicken Stock**
1/4 cup **Soy Sauce**
1/4 cup **Honey**
2 tbsp. **Wine**
2 tbsp. chopped **Onions**

Pork Tenderloin Birds

6 **Pork Tenderloins**
1/2 tsp. **Salt**
Dash of **Pepper**
1/2 to 1 tsp. **Sage** to taste
1 **Egg**, slightly beaten

2 cups **Bread Crumbs**
2 tbsp. chopped **Onions**
2 tbsp. **Butter**
3/4 cup **Boiling Water**

Combine marinade ingredients and marinate meat overnight in refrigerator. Remove from mixture and drain, reserving marinade. Split (or pound) tenderloins until 1/3" thick. Add salt, pepper, sage and onion to bread crumbs. Mix lightly with fork. Add butter to boiling water, and mix with bread crumb mixture just until moistened (but not wet or soggy). Add egg to stuffing mixture.

Spread split (or pounded) pieces with stuffing and tie with strings to form six rolled meat and stuffing birds. Cook over medium coals for one to one and one-half hours, turning frequently. Baste often with remaining marinade.

Tip: *Fat should not be removed from meat before barbequing because it bastes the meat and keeps it moist.*

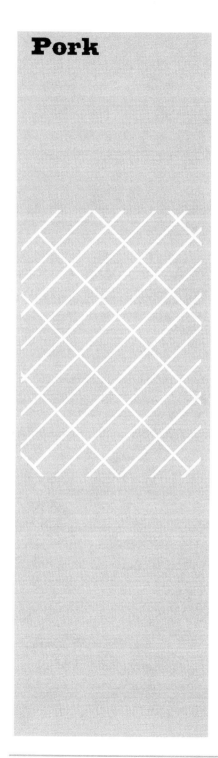

Orange-Glazed Loin Roast

National Pork Producers Council

6 to 8 lb. bone-in **Pork Loin Roast**
1 tbsp. **Dry Mustard**
Salt
Fresh **Ground Pepper**
1/2 can (6 oz.) **Frozen Orange Juice Concentrate**, thawed

1/2 cup **Honey**
2 tbsp. **Steak Sauce**
1 **Orange**, sliced (optional)

Rub dry mustard into roast and sprinkle with salt and pepper. Make a drip pan of aluminum foil about one and one-half inches deep and extending about three inches on each side of roast. Place under roast. Insert meat thermometer in thickest part of roast, not touching bone or fat. Place on grill about six inches above low coals. Close hood of grill. Cook for two to three hours or until meat thermometer registers 160 degrees.

Combine orange juice concentrate, honey, and steak sauce in a small saucepan. Heat until bubbly, and brush on roast. Grill an additional 30 minutes or until meat thermometer registers 170 degrees. Baste often with sauce. Let roast stand for 10 to 15 minutes before carving to allow juices to set. Garnish with orange slices, if desired. Serves 10 to 14.

Mustard Glazed Ham Steaks

National Pork Producers Council

4 boneless **Ham Steaks**
   (cut 1/2-inch thick)
5 tbsp. **Brown Sugar**
1 tbsp. **Dry Mustard**
1 tsp. **Onion Salt**

2 tsp. **Soy Sauce**
2 tsp. **Lemon Juice**
1 cup unsweetened **Pineapple Juice**
1 can (8 oz.) **Pineapple Slices**
   (optional)

Combine brown sugar, dry mustard, onion salt, soy sauce and lemon juice in a small saucepan. Mix until smooth. Add pineapple juice, mixing well. Simmer sauce five minutes, stirring occasionally.

Place ham steaks on grill three to four inches above medium coals. Cook 30 minutes, turning steaks every five minutes and brushing with sauce. Serve steaks with sauce. Garnish with heated pineapple slices, if desired. Makes 4 to 8 servings.

Honey Apple Pork Chops

National Pork Producers Council

4 **Pork Loin Chops** (8 oz. each)
   (about one inch thick)
1 1/2 cups **Apple Cider**
1/4 cup **Lemon Juice**

1/4 cup **Soy Sauce**
2 tbsp. **Honey**
1 clove **Garlic,** minced
1/4 tsp. **Pepper**

Combine all ingredients, EXCEPT pork chops. Mix well. Place chops in a shallow dish; pour marinade over chops. Cover and refrigerate overnight, turning meat occasionally.

Remove pork chops from marinade. Place on grill approximately six inches above low to medium coals. Grill for 40 to 50 minutes, turning and basting with marinade every 10 to 15 minutes. Makes 4 servings.

Tip: Refrigerate pork or store in insulated cooler until ready to grill. Do not interrupt cooking. Partial cooking may encourage bacterial growth before cooking is complete.

Barbecued Pork Roast

Courtesy of The Reynolds Wrap® Kitchens

3 to 4 lbs. **Pork Shoulder Blade**   1/3 cup **Ketchup**
    Boston Roast (boneless)   3 tbsp. **Vinegar**
Salt   1 tbsp. **Mustard**
Pepper   1 tbsp. **Vegetable Oil**
1/4 cup **Sugar**

Season roast with salt and pepper. Insert meat thermometer into thickest part of roast. Grill over medium hot coals using the Indirect Method of heat distribution under Heavy Duty Reynolds Wrap® hood.

In a small saucepan, combine remaining ingredients and simmer five minutes. After one hour, begin basting with barbecue sauce. Baste every 15 minutes. Grill 1 1/2 to 2 hours (or until thermometer reads 170 degrees. Makes 8 to 10 servings.

Note: The Indirect Method of heat distribution is ideal for meats preferred well done. Equal amounts of charcoal are placed on either side of the fire bowl. An aluminum foil drip pan can be placed in the center to catch fat drippings. A cover or hood is used to help provide reflective heat for evenly-cooked foods.

Tip: Defrost frozen pork in the refrigerator. Bacteria can multiply quickly at room temperature and will grow on the meat surface while meat remains frozen inside.

Recipe:_____

From:_____

Ingredients:

_____   _____

_____   _____

_____   _____

_____   _____

_____   _____

Directions:_____

_____

_____

_____

_____

Recipe:_____

From:_____

Ingredients:

_____   _____

_____   _____

_____   _____

_____   _____

_____   _____

Directions:_____

_____

_____

_____

_____

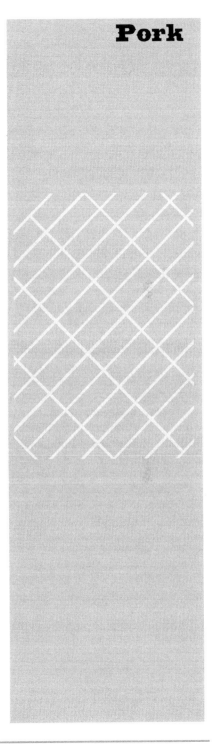

Pork

Pork

Recipe:_____

From:_____

Ingredients:

_____   _____

_____   _____

_____   _____

_____   _____

_____   _____

Directions:_____

_____

_____

_____

_____

Recipe:_____

From:_____

Ingredients:

_____   _____

_____   _____

_____   _____

_____   _____

_____   _____

Directions:_____

_____

_____

_____

_____

Ribs

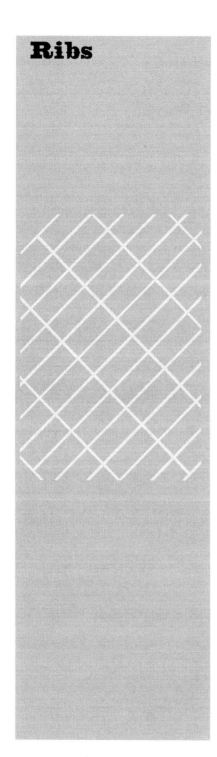

Ribs

Mesquite Broiled Spareribs

Desert Mesquite of Arizona, Inc.

3 to 4 lbs. **Spare Ribs** (country style)
1 cup diced **Celery**
1 medium **Onion**, diced
2 tbsp. **Olive Oil**
1 cup **Ketchup**
1/2 cup **Water**

1 tsp. **White Vinegar**
1/2 cup **Dark Brown Sugar**
2 tsp. **Dry Mustard**
1 tsp. **Worcestershire Sauce**
1/2 tsp. **Garlic Powder**
1/2 tsp. **Pepper**

Barbeque the spareribs on a charcoal or gas grill using Mesquite Wood Barbeque Chips to add the mesquite flavor. If your grill has a cover, use it to capture the smoke from the mesquite wood. It is not necessary to barbeque the ribs until they are well done, since they will be cooked in the barbeque sauce.

While the ribs are being grilled, sauté the onion and celery in the olive oil until the onion is translucent. Add all the remaining ingredients and simmer for 10 minutes. Arrange the ribs in a baking dish, spoon sauce over ribs and bake covered at 300 degrees for one hour (or place ribs in a crock pot, pour sauce over ribs and cook on low heat for five hours or high heat for two and one-half hours). Serve the ribs on a platter with the sauce in a separate dish for spooning over ribs. Serves 6.

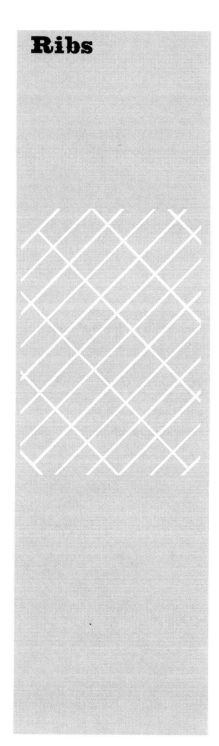

Edna's Bar-B-Q Beef Ribs

Edna Chadsey – Ooltewah, Tennessee

5 lbs. **Beef Ribs** (or short ribs)
1/2 cup **Barbecue Sauce**
  (smoke flavored)
1/2 cup **Soy Sauce**

3 tbsp. **Honey**
1 tsp. **Salt**
1/2 tsp. **Pepper**
1/2 tsp. **Basil**

Put ribs on a rack in shallow roasting pan. Bake 30 minutes in a 325 degree oven. Mix all other ingredients and pour over ribs. Bake for one hour or until well done. Serves 6.

Georgia Spare Ribs

Helen Gordon – Atlanta, Georgia

1 tbsp. **Vinegar**
1 tbsp. **Worcestershire Sauce**
2 tsp. **Salt**
1/2 tsp. **Paprika**
1/4 tsp. **Red Pepper**
1/4 tsp. **Black Pepper**

1 tsp. **Chili Powder**
1/3 cup **Ketchup**
1/3 cup **Water**
2 lbs. **Spare Ribs**
1 **Onion**, sliced

Combine first nine ingredients into a sauce. Put ribs into roaster, top with onion slices. Pour sauce over ribs. Cover and bake in 350 degree oven 1 1/2 hours, basting occasionally. Turn ribs one or two times. Remove cover during final 15 minutes to brown ribs. Serves 2.

Johnnie's Barbecued Spareribs

Mr. & Mrs. Johnnie Davis – Tallahassee, Florida

6 to 8 lbs. lean **Spareribs**
1 cup **Pure Maple Syrup**
1 cup **Ketchup**
1/4 cup **Vinegar**

2 tbsp. **Worcestershire Sauce**
4 tsp. **Onion Salt**
1 tsp. **Chili Powder**
2 tsp. **Dry Mustard**

Cut spareribs into two-rib sections. To make sauce, blend remaining ingredients. Brush the curved side of spareribs with sauce. Arrange in single layer, sauce side down, in shallow baking pan. Brush top of ribs with sauce. Cover with aluminum foil and bake at 375 degrees 45 minutes. Uncover and continue baking about one hour more, or until ribs are tender, brushing about four times with remaining sauce during baking. Makes 10 servings.

Sonny's B-B-Q Ribs

Janet C. Brunner – St. Augustine, Florida

4 lbs. **Spare Ribs**
5 tbsp. **Sugar**
3 tbsp. **Honey**
1 can **Chicken Broth**
3 tbsp. **Soy Sauce**

1 tbsp. **Ketchup**
1 tbsp. **Open Pit® BBQ Sauce**
   (Original Flavor)
1 tsp. **Salt**

Boil the spare ribs for one hour. Skim and drain. Mix the remaining ingredients and pour over ribs in a 9×13 pan. Bake uncovered in a 325 degree oven for three hours.

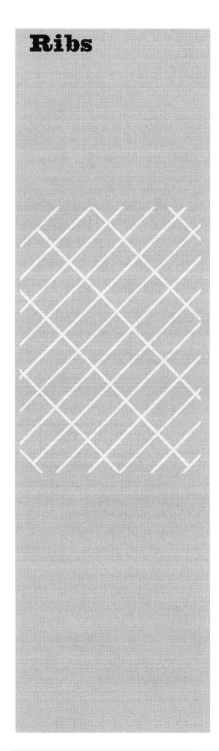

Hickory Country-Style Ribs

National Pork Producers Council

4 lbs. **Pork Country-Style Ribs** (cut into 4-rib portions)
1 1/2 cups **Cooking Oil**
3/4 cup **Soy Sauce**
1/2 cup **Vinegar**
1/4 cup **Worcestershire Sauce**
1/3 cup **Orange Juice**
2 tbsp. **Dry Mustard**
1 tbsp. **Coarse Ground Black Pepper**
2 tsp. **Salt**
2 tbsp. chopped **Fresh Parsley**
2 cloves **Garlic**, minced

Combine all ingredients, EXCEPT ribs, and mix well. Place ribs in a shallow dish, cover with marinade and refrigerate for 24 hours, turning meat occasionally.

Place several pre-soaked hickory chips on hot coals. Remove ribs from marinade and place approximately six inches above coals. Close hood of grill. Cook over low heat for about one hour and fifteen minutes (or until done), brushing occasionally with marinade. Serves 4-6.

Barbecued Pork Ribs with Sam's Special Sauce

Courtesy of Sam Higgins – Texas

1 1/2 quarts **Mesquite Chips**
1/4 cup **Dry Rub**

12 lbs. **Pork Spareribs**
(do not separate ribs)
Sam's Special Sauce

Soak mesquite chips in water to cover for 30 minutes. Drain well.

Dry Rub

1/4 cup **Salt**
1 1/2 tsp. fresh **Ground Black Pepper**

1 1/2 tsp. ground **Red Pepper**

Mix all ingredients in a small bowl. Prepare barbecue grill, lighting fire at one end only. When coals turn white, spread one-third of mesquite over coals. Rub Dry Rub into ribs. Place on grill away from fire. Cover and smoke three hours, maintaining temperature at about 275 degrees, turning ribs every hour. Add more mesquite every hour and sprinkle chips with water occasionally.

Sam's Special Sauce

2 cups **Mustard**
1/2 cup **Beer**

1/2 cup firmly-packed **Light Brown Sugar**
2 1/2 tsp. **Hot Pepper Sauce**

Combine all ingredients. Baste smoked ribs with sauce. Cover and cook until very tender, basting and turning occasionally (about 1 1/2 hours). Cut ribs apart and serve hot.

Note: Sauce can be prepared three days ahead and refrigerated. Makes about three cups of sauce.

Sam Higgins is the co-author of the book I'm Glad I Ate When I Did, 'Cause I'm Not Hungry Now. He is a Texas cook whose classes, catering services and State Fair of Texas winnings have made him a living legend. Mr. Higgins' book is available from the Texas School Book Depository, 8301 Ambassador Row, Dallas, TX 75247.

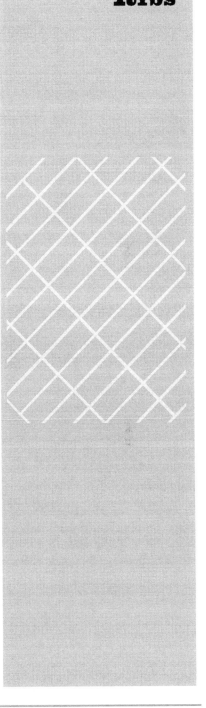

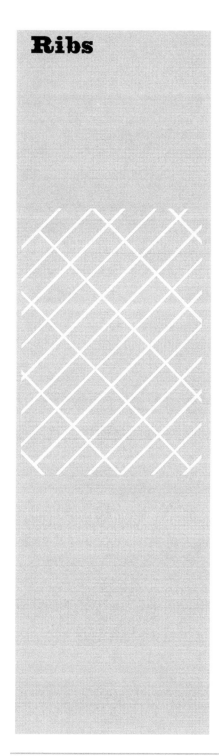

Barbecued Beef Short Ribs

Courtesy The Kingsford® Company

6 lbs. **Beef Chuck Short Ribs** (cut into 1-rib pieces)
3/4 cup **Soy Sauce**
2/3 cup **Dry Sherry**
1/2 cup packed **Dark Brown Sugar**
6 cloves **Garlic**, minced
1 tbsp. **Ground Cayenne Red Pepper**
1 tbsp. fresh grated **Gingerroot**
2 tsp. **Chinese Five Spice Powder**
1 cup **Water**

Trim excess fat from ribs. In a large roasting pan, arrange ribs in a single layer.

For marinade: in a medium saucepan combine soy sauce sherry, brown sugar, garlic, red pepper, gingerroot, five spice powder, and water. Cook over medium heat until sugar is dissolved. Remove from heat; cool slightly. Pour marinade over ribs. Cover and marinate in refrigerator for two hours, turning ribs once.

Cover roasting pan with foil. In a covered grill, arrange medium-hot Kingsford® briquets for indirect cooking of ribs. Place roasting pan on grill rack. Cover grill and cook ribs for 45 minutes. Remove foil from roasting pan and continue cooking in covered grill 45 to 60 minutes more (or until ribs are tender), turning ribs occasionally. Brush ribs again with marinade just before serving. Serves 8.

Rose's Barbecued Spareribs

Rose Cepeck – Green Valley, Arizona

Butter and **Flour** (for browning)
4 lbs. **Spareribs**
2 medium **Onions**, diced
1 **Green Pepper**, diced
1 tbsp. **Salt**

1 tsp. **Pepper**
1 cup **Ketchup**
2 tbsp. **Horseradish**
1 1/2 cups **Water**

Cut spareribs in small pieces and roll in flour. Brown quickly in butter heated to sizzling in roaster. Combine all ingredients in saucepan and simmer 10 minutes. Pour over ribs in roaster on 325 degree heat for one hour.

Country Style Ribs

Bob Durbin – New Braunfels, Texas

1 cup **Ketchup**
1/3 cup **Worcestershire Sauce**
1 tsp. **Chili Powder**
2 dashes **Tabasco® Pepper Sauce**

1 tsp. **Salt**
2 cups **Water**
3 to 4 lbs. **Pork Ribs** (country style)
1 large **Onion**

Combine ketchup, Worcestershire, chili powder, Tabasco®, salt and water in medium saucepan and bring to boil. Simmer, covered, for 20 to 30 minutes. Place ribs in shallow roasting pan (Teflon pan will clean easier). Pour sauce over ribs covering about 2/3 of the ribs. Slice onion and place over ribs. Spoon sauce over ribs and place roasting pan on grill (high heat if using charcoal). Turn every 10-15 minutes, spooning sauce over ribs. As sauce boils down and thickens, continue spooning over ribs. Allow about one hour to cook ribs. If sauce boils down too quickly, add more sauce.

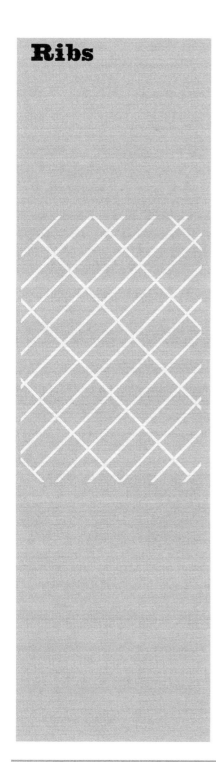

Oriental Spareribs

Courtesy of A-1® Steak Sauce

3 tbsp. **A-1® Steak Sauce**
1 cup bottled **Barbecue Sauce**
1/4 cup **All Purpose Soy Sauce**
1/4 cup **Sherry Cooking Wine**
3 lbs. **Country Style Spareribs**

In plastic bag, combine A-1®, barbecue sauce, soy sauce and sherry. Add spareribs. Seal tightly with twist tie. Marinate several hours or overnight. Drain. Grill spareribs on both sides basting and turning occasionally, 30-45 minutes or until cooked through. Serves 4-6.

Hot and Spicy Spare Ribs

National Pork Producers Council

2 tbsp. **Butter** or **Margarine**
1 medium **Onion**, finely chopped
2 cloves **Garlic**, minced
1 can (15 oz.) **Tomato Sauce**
2/3 cup **Cider Vinegar**
2/3 cup firmly packed **Brown Sugar**
2 tbsp. **Chili Powder**
1 tbsp. **Mustard**
1/2 tsp. **Pepper**
1 rack (3 lb.) **Pork Spareribs**

Melt butter in a large skillet over low heat. Add onions and garlic and sauté until tender. Add remaining ingredients, EXCEPT ribs, and bring to a boil. Reduce heat, and simmer for 20 minutes, stirring occasionally.

In a hooded grill, place a large piece of aluminum foil over coals beneath grill to catch drippings. Baste meatiest side of ribs with sauce. Place ribs on grill, meatiest side down, about six inches above low coals. Baste top side. Close grill hood. Cook about 20 minutes. Turn ribs and baste. Cook an additional 45 minutes or until done, basting every 10 to 15 minutes with sauce. Serves 3-4.

Glaze for Ribs

Martha Hacon – Atlanta, Georgia

3 lbs. **Spare Ribs**
4 tbsp. **Soy Sauce**
1/4 tsp. fresh **Ground Black Pepper**

3 drops **Tabasco® Pepper Sauce**
1 1/2 cups **Honey**

Cut spareribs into serving-size pieces. Put ribs into a roasting pan.

Combine soy sauce, pepper, Tabasco® and spread over meat. Pour on honey. Let ribs stand for one-half hour. Turn ribs over and baste thoroughly with sauce. Let stand for another half-hour.

Roast in 350 degree oven for one hour and twenty minutes. Turn and baste occasionally while cooking. Makes 4 servings.

Easy Barbecued Spareribs

Gail S. Thomas – White Hall, Maryland

3 lbs. **Spare Ribs**
1 bottle (14 oz.) **Ketchup**
1 1/4 cups **Water**
1/4 cup **Vinegar**
3 tbsp. **Brown Sugar**

1 tbsp. **Dry Mustard**
3 tbsp. **Worcestershire Sauce**
2 tsp. **Chili Powder**
Pinch **Cloves**
Pinch **Garlic Powder**

Cut ribs into serving-size pieces. Place in a 13×9×2 baking pan. Bake at 400 degrees for 30 minutes. Combine remaining ingredients and mix well. Spoon over ribs. Reduce heat to 350 degrees. Bake an additional 1 1/2 hours, or until tender. Serves 3 to 4.

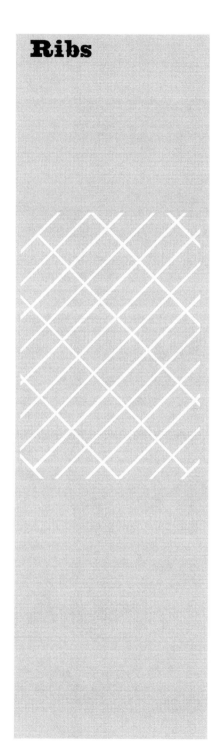

Maple-Mustard-Glazed Spareribs

National Pork Producers Council

4 lbs. **Pork Spareribs**
1/2 tsp. **Salt**
1/2 tsp. **Mixed Pickling Spice**
1 small **Onion**, coarsely chopped
2 tbsp. **Cooking Oil**
1/2 to 2/3 cup **Pure Maple Syrup**

1/4 cup **Vinegar**
2 tbsp. **Water**
1 tbsp. **Dijon-style Mustard**
Dash **Salt**
1/4 tsp. fresh **Ground Pepper**

Sprinkle spareribs with 1/2 teaspoon salt. Tie pickling spice in several thicknesses of cheesecloth to make a bouquet garni* and set aside.

For glaze, in a saucepan cook onion in hot oil until tender. Add the bouquet garni. Stir in syrup, vinegar, water, mustard, dash salt and pepper and simmer 20 minutes. Discard bouquet garni.

Make a foil drip pan, if desired. Arrange slow coals on both sides of drip pan. Place ribs on grill. Lower grill hood or cover with foil tent. Grill ribs about one hour until done. During last 20 minutes of cooking, brush ribs occasionally with glaze. Serves 3-4.

Hint: *A bouquet garni is defined as several herbs bundled together in a cheesecloth and used to flavor dishes. They can be removed easily before the dish is served.

Barbecued Short Ribs

Alice Hogan – Dallas, Texas

5 lbs. **Lean Beef Short Ribs**
   (3-4 inches long)
1/4 cup **Salad Oil**
1/4 cup **Soy Sauce**
1/4 cup **Wine Vinegar**
1/4 cup **Orange Marmalade**

2 tbsp. **Worcestershire Sauce**
1 tbsp. **Dried Mustard**
1 tsp. **Dried Parsley Flakes**
1 tsp. **Garlic Salt**
1/2 tsp. **Lemon Pepper**

Place short ribs in large bowl. Combine remaining ingredients and pour over ribs. Cover and refrigerate eight to ten hours (or overnight), turning occasionally. Remove from marinade and drain thoroughly. Cook slowly on grill seven to eight inches from coals, for about two hours (or until meat begins to leave bone), turning frequently. Brush with marinade during last 20 minutes of cooking time. Serves 6.

Glazed Spareribs

Calvin E. Ayers – Baltimore, Maryland

1/2 cup **Ketchup**
1/4 cup **Mustard**
1/4 cup **Cider Vinegar**
1 tbsp. **Hot Sauce** (optional)

1/2 tsp. **Powdered Ginger**
1/4 cup **Dark Corn Syrup**
4 to 6 lbs. **Ribs**
1 medium **Onion**, sliced

Mix first six ingredients and pour over ribs. Refrigerate for two hours. Remove ribs from marinade. Cover with sliced onions, baste with marinade and bake at 350 degrees for two hours. Turn ribs occasionally, basting with sauce. Serves 4.

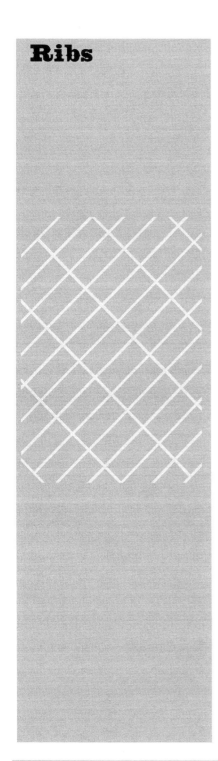

Maui Marinated Beef Shortribs

Hawaii Ginger Industry Association

2 tbsp. **Sesame Seeds**
1 tbsp. **Butter** or **Margarine**
1 cup **Soy Sauce**
3/4 cup **Red Wine**
1/2 cup **Red Wine Vinegar**
4 **Green Onions**, trimmed and
    coarsely chopped

1 medium **Onion**, coarsely chopped
2 large cloves **Garlic**, minced
1 1/2 tbsp. **Brown Sugar**
1 tbsp. **Vegetable Oil**
2 tsp. fresh minced **Hawaiian**
    Ginger Root
4 to 5 lbs. **Lean Beef Shortribs**
    (cut in 2-inch lengths)

Combine sesame seeds and butter. Cook until just starting to turn brown. Combine remaining ingredients (EXCEPT for ribs), add to sesame seed mixture and simmer until well blended. Place ribs in pan, cover with sauce and marinate overnight. Barbeque over low flame on grill. Brush with sauce while cooking.

Sweet 'n Sour Spareribs

Courtesy of A.1.® Steak Sauce

3 lbs. **Spareribs**
3 tbsp. **A.1.**® **Steak Sauce**
1 cup bottled **Barbecue Sauce**

2/3 cup **Apricot Preserves**
2 tbsp. **Lemon Juice**

On rack in pan, bake spareribs in 350 degree oven one hour. Cut into serving size pieces. Combine remaining ingredients for sauce. Grill spareribs, basting generously with sauce, turning frequently, 15-20 minutes or until well glazed. Serves 4-6.

Down South Barbecued Ribs

Alden J. Thorson – Spring Hill, Florida

4 lbs. **Spare Ribs** (or country style ribs)
1 1/2 cups light unsulphured **Molasses**
3/4 cup **Lemon Juice**
4 tbsp. **A.1.® Sauce**

4 tbsp. **Worcestershire Sauce**
3 cloves **Garlic**, minced well
Salt and **Pepper** to taste

Divide ribs into racks of two ribs each. Place in a shallow dish and marinate overnight in the refrigerator (or two to three hours at room temperature). Combine molasses, lemon juice, A.1.® Sauce, Worcestershire Sauce, and garlic and cover ribs. Remove ribs from marinade and drain well. Salt and pepper to taste. Place ribs on grill about six inches above gray coals. Baste well with sauce. Turn ribs every eight or ten minutes, basting each time until crispy and done. Serves 4.

Sierra Ranch Ribs

Courtesy Best Foods – New Jersey

4 lbs. country-style **Spare Ribs**
Water
1 can (8 oz.) **Tomato Sauce**
1 cup chopped **Onion**
1/2 cup **Karo® Dark Corn Syrup**

1/4 cup **Cider Vinegar**
2 tbsp. **Worcestershire Sauce**
1 tsp. **Salt**
1 tsp. **Dry Mustard**
1/2 tsp. **Chili Powder**

Trim spare ribs and cut into serving pieces. Place ribs in a five-quart saucepan. Add water to depth of one inch and cover. Bring to boil over high heat; reduce heat and boil gently one hour (or until ribs are fork tender). In a one-quart saucepan mix remaining ingredients. Bring to a boil. Reduce heat and simmer 10 minutes. Drain ribs. Brush generously with sauce. Grill ribs six inches from heat, basting and turning frequently (about 15 minutes or until browned). Or broil four inches from heat, basting occasionally and turning once (about 20 minutes). If desired, heat remaining sauce and serve with ribs. Serves 6.

Indoor Barbequed Spareribs

Joan Halper – Tucson, AZ.

4 to 5 lbs. **Ribs**
3 tsp. **Salt**
1/2 tsp. **Black Pepper**
1/2 tsp. **Chili Powder**
1/2 tsp. **Paprika**
1/2 tsp. **Poultry Seasoning**

1 large **Onion**
2 cans (8 oz.) **Tomato Sauce**
2 cups **Water**
2 tsp. **Sugar**

Trim excess fat from spareribs. Place them in one or two shallow baking pans, so that ribs are in a single layer.

In a bowl, combine spices and seasonings. Sprinkle both sides of ribs with the mixture. Slice onion over top of ribs and pour on tomato sauce. Add water and sprinkle on sugar.

Bake at 325 degrees for 2 1/2 hours or until very tender. Baste and turn ribs several times during cooking. Sauce should be thick (but add more water if needed). Serves 4-6.

Quickie Cajun Ribs

Barbecue Industry Association

1 cup bottled tomato-based
Barbecue Sauce
1 tbsp. **Honey**
1/2 tsp. **Onion Powder**
1/2 tsp. **Garlic Powder**
1/2 tsp. fresh **Ground Black Pepper**

1/2 tsp. dried **Oregano Leaves**
1/4 tsp. **Cayenne Pepper**
1/4 tsp. **Hot Pepper Sauce** (or to taste)
4 to 6 lbs. **Pork Back Ribs**
Salt

Prepare a medium-hot charcoal fire. Combine all ingredients (EXCEPT for ribs and salt) in a small saucepan and set aside.

Season ribs with salt and place bone-side down on an oiled cooking grid set four to six inches above ashed coals.

Grill, turning once or twice, until lightly browned (about 20 to 25 minutes).

Meanwhile, place the pot of barbecue sauce on the side of the cooking grid to warm. Brush ribs with sauce and continue turning and brushing until meat is well-browned and cooked thoroughly (about 15 minutes longer).

Cut slabs of ribs into serving portions. Serves 6.

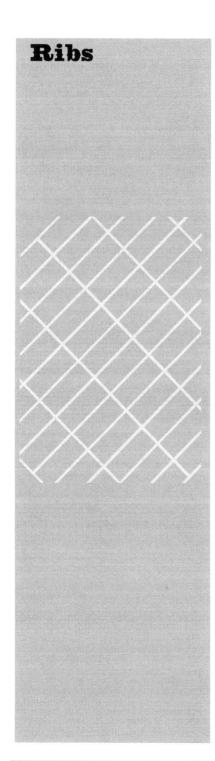

Derby Day Ribs

John Brownlee – Conway, Arkansas

8 lbs. **Ribs** (country style)
1 bottle (12 oz.) **Reese's® Teriyaki Sauce**
1 bottle (10oz.) **Kikkoman® Soy Sauce**
2 cups **Chablis**
1 stick (1/4 lb.) **Butter** or **Margarine**

Parboil ribs for one hour (20 minutes if using pressure cooker). Combine teriyaki sauce, soy sauce and Chablis. Place ribs in a shallow pan. Pour sauce mixture over ribs. Cover and marinate overnight in refrigerator. Remove ribs and pour marinade into saucepan. Add butter and heat until melted, stirring well. Cook ribs over "slow" charcoal fire for approximately 30 minutes, basting frequently with sauce. Serves 10.

Arizona Style Barbecued Ribs

Agri-Business Council – Phoenix, Arizona

8 to 10 lbs. **Country-style Pork Ribs**

Brown ribs in heavy skillet, then place on broiling pan. Cover with foil and bake two to three hours (or until tender). Transfer ribs to large baking pan, pour barbecue sauce over ribs and bake two hours at 350 degrees. Serves 20 at two ribs per person.

Use "**Aunt Polly's Barbecue Sauce**" (see page 115) or your favorite.

Aunt Polly's Barbecue Sauce

Courtesy Susan Nunn, Tempe, Arizona

1 can (28 oz.) **Tomatoes**
2 large **Onions**, chopped
5 oz. **Worcestershire Sauce**
1 can (15 1/2 oz.) **Crushed Pineapple**, drained
1/2 cup (or more) **Molasses** or **Honey** to taste
Fresh **Ground Pepper** to taste
1 bottle (28 oz.) **Hickory-flavored Barbecue Sauce**

In crockery slow cooker, combine ingredients, (except for Barbecue Sauce) breaking up canned tomatoes with a spoon. Add bottled barbecue sauce and simmer for about five hours.

Shortcreek Barbecued Ribs

William Patterson – Flagstaff, Arizona

3 lbs. **Short Ribs**
2 tbsp. **Lard**
1 medium **Onion**, minced
1/4 cup **Vinegar**
2 tbsp. **Brown Sugar**
1 cup **Ketchup**
1/2 cup **Water**
3 tbsp. **Worcestershire Sauce** (optional)
1 tsp. **Mustard**
1/2 cup diced **Celery**
2 tsp. **Salt**

Cut ribs into sections two or three inches long. Brown in lard. Add onion and brown. Add remaining ingredients to pan. Cover and cook slowly on top of stove (or bake in 350 degree oven from one to two hours until tender). Serves 4.

Spicy Spareribs Barbecue

Barbara Thomas – Ooltewah, Tennessee

1 envelope **Dry Onion Soup Mix**
1 1/2 cups **Water**
1/3 cup **Honey**
1/4 cup **Soy Sauce**
2 tbsp. **Sherry**
1 tbsp. **Sugar**
1 clove **Garlic**, minced
1 tsp. **Ginger**
4 lbs. **Spare Ribs** (cut into
    1 or 2 rib portions)

Mix first eight ingredients in large bowl. Add ribs and marinate two hours, turning often. Preheat oven to 350 degrees. Put ribs on rack in shallow roasting pan. Roast 1 1/4 hours or until tender. Turn and baste several times with marinade. Serves 6.

Donna's Barbecued Ribs

Donna Arnold – San Pablo, California

3 lbs. **Ribs** (cut in pieces)
1 to 2 tbsp. **Liquid Smoke**
1 cup **Ketchup**
1/4 cup **Worcestershire Sauce**
1/4 cup **Lemon Juice** (or sliced lemon)
1 tsp. **Salt**
1 tsp. **Chili Powder**
1 cup **Water**
1 tsp. **Celery Seed**

Place ribs in shallow pan, meaty side up. Brush ribs with liquid smoke. Roast in 450 degree oven for 30 minutes. Combine remaining ingredients in a saucepan, heat to boiling and pour over ribs. Reduce oven heat to 350 degrees and continue baking for one hour. Baste with sauce every 15 to 20 minutes. Serves 5.

Tip: To parboil ribs, bring water to a boil, cut the ribs into serving pieces, drop them into the boiling water and simmer, covered, for 45 minutes (or until done). Ribs can then be grilled (5 minutes to a side) and served with sauce.

Barbecued Pork Spareribs, India

Sister M. Blanche Aubuchon – Tucson, AZ.

12 lbs. **Spareribs** (cut apart in sections of 2 bones each)
2 cans **Beer** (room temperature)
Salt and **Pepper**

Place ribs in large Dutch oven or two flat pans. Bake in 325 degree oven for three hours (or longer, in order to be well done). After 45 minutes, pour on beer. Half an hour later, salt and pepper lightly, and start to baste occasionally with sauce. Be sure all pieces are basted, and do not let ribs get too brown or burn. Shield with aluminum foil, if necessary. When done, pan drippings may be thickened for gravy.

Sauce for Spareribs, India

1 cup **Honey**
1 cup **Apple Cider Vinegar**
1 cup **Mustard**
1 cup **Apricot Jam**
1 tsp. **Powdered Ginger**
2 tbsp. **Curry Powder**
1 **Onion**, finely minced

Mix well and drizzle on ribs (or apply with pastry brush). If ribs are not browned, uncover the last 15 minutes and turn heat up a little. Serves 20.

Tip: After adding starter fuel, wait about one minute before lighting the dampened coals, so the fluid can vaporize into gas.

Sparerib Ticklers

By Permission: Lea & Perrins,® Inc.

3 lbs. **Pork Spareribs** (cut into serving pieces)
1 1/2 cups **Chili Sauce**
1/3 cup **Lea & Perrins® Worcestershire Sauce**
1/2 cup finely chopped **Onion**
1/2 cup finely chopped **Green Pepper**

Preheat oven to 400 degrees. Place spareribs on a rack in a foil-lined baking pan. Bake until almost tender (about 40 minutes), turning after 20 minutes.

Meanwhile, prepare sauce by combining in a small saucepan chili sauce, Lea & Perrins® Worcestershire Sauce, onion and green pepper. Bring to a boil. Reduce heat and simmer, covered, for 20 minutes.

Remove pan from oven. Brush ribs with sauce. Return to oven until ribs are tender (about 20 minutes), turning and brushing with sauce occasionally.

To cook on a grill, brush baked ribs with sauce. Place on a rack over hot coals until ribs are tender and glazed (about 20 minutes), turning and brushing often with sauce. (This sauce can also be used for beef or chicken.) Yield: 4 to 6 portions, 2 3/4 cups sauce.

Tip: Line the grill firebox with heavy-duty aluminum foil and about an inch of gravel. The gravel acts as an insulator to keep the fire hotter.

Mom Mac's Barbecued Ribs

Patricia Myers – Food Editor,
The Arizona Republic and The Phoenix Gazette

3 lbs. **Spareribs** (or country-style ribs)
1 can (8oz.) **Tomato Sauce** or
   1 cup **Ketchup**
1 can (or 1 cup) **Water**
2 tbsp. **Brown Sugar**
2 tbsp. **Vinegar**
2 tbsp. **Worcestershire Sauce**

2 **Onions**, sliced
1 tsp. **Salt**
1/4 tsp. **Pepper**
1 tsp. (or more) **Paprika**
Dash **Cayenne Pepper**
Liquid Hickory Smoke Flavoring
  (optional)

Pre-cook the ribs in a slow-cooker for 3 to 4 hours. Transfer ribs to outdoor heated grill. Combine all ingredients and brush on sauce at 10-minute intervals.

This recipe can also be prepared in a slow-cooker or oven.

SLOW-COOKER: Brown meat and season, then place in cooker. Combine other ingredients and pour over. Cook on low for 6 to 10 hours, or on high for 4 to 5 hours. To thicken sauce, remove lid during last half-hour or hour of cooking.

OVEN: bake in a covered cast-iron Dutch oven at 325 degrees for 1 to 1 1/2 hours, basting occasionally.

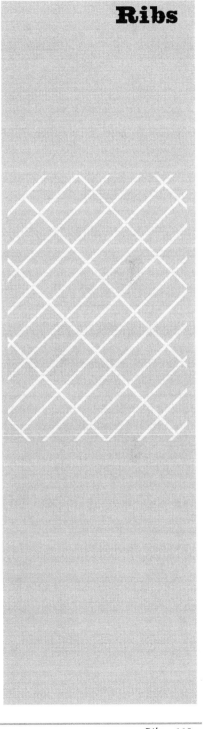

Ribs

Recipe:_____

From:_____

Ingredients:

_____   _____

_____   _____

_____   _____

_____   _____

_____   _____

Directions:_____

_____

_____

_____

_____

Recipe:_____

From:_____

Ingredients:

_____   _____

_____   _____

_____   _____

_____   _____

_____   _____

Directions:_____

_____

_____

_____

_____

Wild Game and Variety Meats

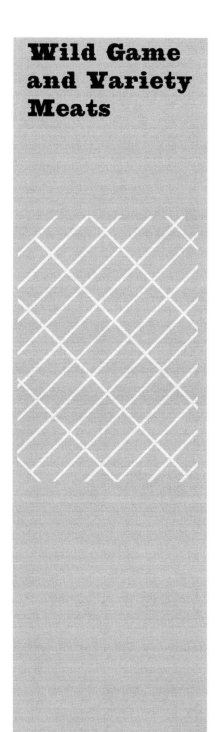

Wild Game and Variety Meats

Road-Runner Bar-B-Q Venison

Bob Roberts – Taylor, Texas

1 **Deer Ham** (5 or 6 lbs.) or leg of lamb or goat
3 or 4 cloves **Garlic** (sliced into small slivers)
2 or 3 canned **Jalapeno Peppers**, sliced into small slivers
2 tsp. **Salt**
2 tbsp. **Pepper**

Wash meat with water and pat dry with paper towel. With point of paring knife, make small slits in meat (about one-half-inch deep), as if preparing a ham for whole cloves. Insert garlic slivers into meat slits, alternating with jalapeno bits. Rub meat with salt and pepper.

Basting Sauce

1 cup **Red Wine**
2/3 cup **Cider Vinegar**
Juice from 2 **Limes** (or 2 lemons)
3 cups **Hot Water**

1 stick **Butter** or **Margarine**
2 cloves **Garlic**, pressed
1 tbsp. **Salt**
2 tbsp. **Pepper**

Combine all ingredients in saucepan, mix well and heat.

Place meat on grill over low charcoal fire and baste with sauce every 15 to 20 minutes. Keep sauce hot while basting and stir sauce frequently. Cook until meat is tender, about four or five hours. Serves 8 to 10.

Turkey Barbecue

Juanita E. Bosecker – Saint Louis, Missouri

3 **Turkey Drumsticks** (fresh or frozen)
1 medium **Onion**, chopped
2 tbsp. **Butter**
2 tbsp. **Vinegar**
2 tbsp. **Brown Sugar** (optional)
1 cup **Ketchup**

3 tbsp. **Worcestershire Sauce**
4 tbsp. **Lemon Juice**
1/2 tbsp. **Mustard**
1/2 cup **Water**
1/3 cup chopped **Celery**

Thaw drumsticks (if frozen), salt and bake in 350 degree oven for two hours. (Put water in bottom of turkey roasting pan and cover. This will keep turkey moist and will not require basting.) When cool, de-bone. In saucepan, brown onions in butter, add other ingredients and cook slowly for 30 minutes. Put roasted drumsticks in sauce, stir and heat slowly. Sauce will be absorbed by turkey. Serves 6.

Barbecued Lamb Chops

American Lamb Council – Denver, Colorado

1/4 cup **Cooking Oil**
2 tbsp. **Honey**
2 tbsp. **Soy Sauce**
2 tbsp. **Cider Vinegar** or
     Dry White Wine
2 tbsp. minced **Onion**

1/2 tsp. **Salt**
1/8 tsp. **Pepper**
1/4 tsp. **Ginger**
1/4 tsp. **Dry Mustard**
8 **Lamb Loin** or **Rib Chops**
     (or 4 shoulder chops)

In small bowl, mix together all ingredients except lamb chops. Brush lamb chops generously with sauce and let stand one hour. Grill chops six to seven inches from hot coals for 12 to 15 minutes per side (or until desired doneness), brushing frequently with sauce. Serve chops with remaining sauce. Serves 4.

Barbecued Veal Balls

Harriet Jordan – Wickenburg, Arizona

3/4 lb. **Veal Shoulder** (or neck), ground
1/2 lb. ground **Pork Shoulder**
1 tsp. **Salt**
1 tbsp. minced **Onion**
1/2 cup dry **Bread Crumbs**
1/2 cup **Milk**
1 **Egg**, beaten

Mix all ingredients together and form into balls. Place in baking pan, cover with barbecue sauce and bake in moderate oven (375 degrees) for about 25 minutes. Serves 4.

Ranch Barbecue Sauce

1/3 cup **Dill Pickle Juice**
1/3 cup **Chili Sauce**
2 tsp. **Worcestershire Sauce**
1/2 tsp. **Salt**
3 tbsp. diced **Dill Pickle**
2 drops **Tabasco® Pepper Sauce**

Mix all ingredients together and serve with Barbecued Veal Balls.

Barbecued Deer Meat

Wanda M. Smith – Drakes Branch, Virginia

2 to 3 lbs. **Deer Meat**
2 small **Onions**
6 strips **Bacon**
1 bottle **Barbecue Sauce**
Salt and **Pepper**

Place deer meat in baking dish. Slice onions and spread on meat. Lay bacon strips across meat. Salt and pepper to taste. Pour three-fourths cup barbecue sauce over entire dish. Cover baking dish and bake at 350 degrees for 2 1/2 to 3 hours (or until bacon has cooked to pieces). Baste meat frequently during cooking with remaining sauce. Serves 6.

Grilled Shoulder of Lamb

American Lamb Council – Denver, Colorado

1 **Shoulder of Lamb** (boned, rolled and tied)
1/2 cup **Honey**
1/2 cup **Dry White Wine**
1/2 cup chopped fine **Onion**
1/2 cup chopped fine **Fresh Mint** or 1 tbsp. **Dried Mint**
1 tsp. **Salt**
1/4 tsp. **Ground Pepper**

Place lamb in glass dish. In one-quart bowl, combine remaining ingredients and pour over lamb. Cover with plastic wrap. Refrigerate several hours or overnight. Place lamb on spit over gray hot coals. Grill lamb about one hour (or until meat thermometer registers about 140 degrees for rare, 160 degrees for medium or 170 degrees for well-done), brushing occasionally with marinade. Slice lamb, heat marinade and pour over slices. Serves 6.

Tip: To add coals to a dying fire (or for cooking larger cuts of meats which require longer cooking times) add coals one at a time to edge of fire. As long as the edges of new briquettes are touching burning coals, they will ignite. DO NOT ADD MORE LIGHTER FLUID.

Barbecued Javelina

David L. Phares – Chandler, Arizona

2 to 3 lbs. **Javelina**
1 1/2 cups of a favorite
  Barbecue Sauce
1/2 can **El Pato® Hot Tomato Sauce**

1 **White Onion**
1 **Tomato**
Seasoning Salt
1 **Green Pepper** (optional)

Cut the meat into two-inch cubes. Place the meat in a brown-and-serve bag, adding one cup of the barbecue sauce and one-quarter can of the tomato sauce. Include one slice of onion, separated by rings. Dice one-quarter of the tomato and include in the bag. Add one teaspoon of seasoning salt and two rings of green pepper.

Squeeze as much air out of the bag as possible. Seal and place in either a crock pot or casserole dish. If using the crock pot, set the heat for low. If using the dish and oven, set the oven at 175 degrees.

Allow to cook for at least eight hours. (If you have closer to three pounds of meat, allow it to cook from 9 p.m. all night until 7 a.m. the next morning.)

When finished, drain the sauce and replace with remaining unused barbecue and tomato sauce. Either reheat for one hour and serve, or freeze for later use. When meat has been thawed, reheat slowly in bag in oven or pan of hot water. Serves 6.

Tip: Different woods impart distinctive flavors during barbequing: mesquite for slightly sweet, hickory for tangy smoky, and cherry for mild smoky.

Barbequed Rabbit

Pel-Freez® Rabbit Meat Inc.
www.pel-freez.com

1 box **Pel-Freez® Rabbit Meat** (thawed)
1 1/2 cups **Barbecue Sauce***

Cook rabbit on grill 45 minutes to one hour, basting frequently with sauce. Or, place rabbit in a buttered casserole in a 350 degree oven. Cover with sauce and bake in oven for one hour, covered with lid. Uncover and bake 30 minutes longer—or until tender—adding more sauce as needed. Serves 4.

*Barbecue Sauce

1 1/2 tbsp. **Vinegar**
1 tbsp. **Sugar**
1 1/2 tbsp. **Dry Mustard**
3 tbsp. **Worcestershire Sauce**
1/2 bottle **Chili Sauce**
1 tsp. **Salt**

1 tsp. **Black Pepper**
1 can **Beef Bouillon**
1 medium **Onion**, sliced
2 cloves **Garlic**, minced
1/4 cup melted **Butter**
4 or 5 drops **Liquid Smoke**

Mix all ingredients to blend.

Tip: Liquid smoke can become overpowering, so use it sparingly.

Best-Ever Brunswick Stew

North Carolina Pork Producers Association

1 lb. **Country Ham**, chopped
2 lbs. ground **Chuck**
1 large **Hen**
2 pods **Hot Pepper**
1 small bottle **Ketchup**
2 quarts **Tomatoes**, crushed
1 can (6 oz.) **Tomato Paste**
1 can (10 3/4 oz.) **Tomato Soup**
Dash of **Worcestershire Sauce**
Hot Sauce

Salt and **Pepper** to taste
1/2 lb. **Butter**
2 packages **Green Giant**® frozen **Shoepeg White Corn**
2 packages frozen **Butter Beans**
2 packages frozen **Green Beans**
4 large **Onions**, sliced
1 large package **Great Northern White Beans**, cooked, drained and mashed, (optional)
8 large Potatoes, cooked and mashed

Cook the ham, chuck and hen together in a large stewing pot until tender. Add the pepper pods. Remove chicken from pot and bone. Cut into small pieces and return to pot.

Add ketchup, tomatoes, tomato paste, tomato soup, Worcestershire, hot sauce, salt and pepper to taste. Add butter, corn, beans, and onions. Cook over low heat for 1 1/2 hours, stirring occasionally. Add white beans and potatoes. Makes 8 quarts.

Wild Game and Variety Meats

Recipe:_____
From:_____
Ingredients:

_____   _____
_____   _____
_____   _____
_____   _____
_____   _____

Directions:_____
_____
_____
_____
_____

Recipe:_____
From:_____
Ingredients:

_____   _____
_____   _____
_____   _____
_____   _____

Directions:_____
_____
_____
_____
_____

Kabobs

Kabobs

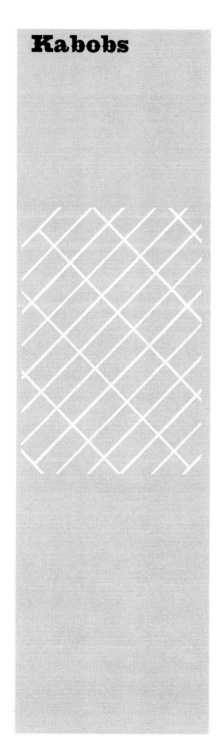

Meatball Kabobs

By Permission Lea & Perrins®, Inc.

1/2 lb. **Ground Beef**
1 **Egg**, lightly beaten
1/2 cup plain **Dry Bread Crumbs**
1 tbsp. **Lea & Perrins®**
   Worcestershire Sauce
1/2 tsp. **Salt**
1/2 tsp. **Garlic Powder**
2 tbsp. **Lea & Perrins®**
   Worcestershire Sauce

1 tbsp. **Vegetable Oil**
1 tsp. **Onion Powder**
1 tsp. **Lemon Juice**
1 1/2 cups **Zucchini**, cut in
   1/4-inch slices
1 cup **Tomato Wedges**
1 cup quartered or halved
   Fresh Mushrooms,

In a small bowl, mix beef, egg, crumbs, one tablespoon Worcestershire sauce, salt and garlic powder. Shape mixture into 18 one-inch meatballs.

Prepare sauce by combining two tablespoons Worcestershire sauce with oil, onion powder and lemon juice.

Place meatballs on six 8-inch skewers alternately with vegetables. Place skewers on a rack over hot coals. Brush with sauce. Cook for 10 minutes, turning and brushing often with sauce. Makes 6 portions.

Tip: To remove grease and grilled-on food particles, sprinkle dry baking soda on a damp sponge and scour, then rinse with a water and baking soda solution.

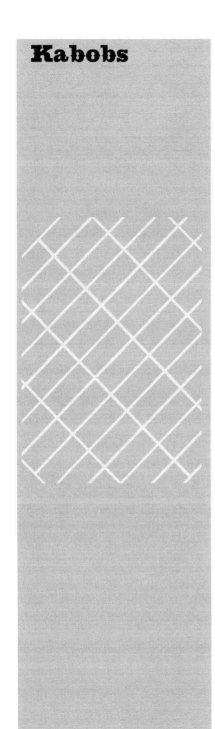

Santa Fe Beef Kabobs

Barbecue Industry Association

2 1/2 lbs. **Boneless Beef** (top round, trimmed of fat and cut into 1 1/2-inch cubes)
2 tbsp. **Olive Oil**
2 tbsp. **Lime Juice**

1 tbsp. **Chili Powder**
1 tsp. **Cumin**
2 cloves **Garlic**, peeled and minced

Prepare a hot charcoal fire. In a large bowl, combine beef cubes with remaining ingredients, tossing to coat evenly.

Thread meat on skewers and grill, turning several times, four to six inches above ashed coals until meat is browned outside and tender, pink and juicy inside, about 10 minutes. Serves 6.

Note: If you are using bamboo skewers, soak the skewers in water for one hour to prevent burning.

Kebab Beef Teriyakis

Weston W. Ross – La Puente, CA

1/2 cup **Pineapple Juice**
1/4 cup **Soy Sauce**
1 clove **Garlic**, sliced
3/4 tsp. **Ginger**

1 lb. **Sirloin Steak**
Canned **Pineapple Chunks**, drained
Stuffed Olives

Combine juice, soy sauce, garlic and ginger. Cut steak into cubes the size of pineapple chunks. Pour marinade over meat and let stand several hours in refrigerator. Alternate meat cubes with pineapple chunks and olives on skewer. Broil about three inches from glowing coals, turning once, 10 to 12 minutes. Serve hot.

Javanese Pork Sate

National Pork Producers Council

1 lb. **Boneless Pork Loin**
2 tbsp. **Peanut Butter**
1/2 cup minced **Onion**
1 clove **Garlic**, minced
2 tbsp. **Lemon Juice**

2 tbsp. **Soy Sauce**
1 tbsp. **Brown Sugar**
Dash **Hot Pepper Sauce**
1 tbsp. **Cooking Oil**

Cut pork into one-half-inch cubes. Blend remaining ingredients together (a blender does this well).

Marinate pork in mixture for 10-15 minutes.

Thread pork on skewers and grill over hot coals for eight to ten minutes, turning occasionally, until done. Serves 4.

Note: If using bamboo skewers, soak skewers in water for one hour to prevent burning.

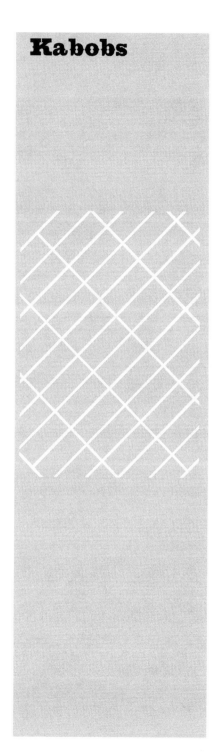

Scallop (or Shrimp) Kabobs

Hickory Specialties, Inc. – Brentwood, Tennessee

1 lb. **Scallops** (or shrimp), fresh or frozen
1 can (13 1/2 oz.) **Pineapple Chunks**, drained
8 oz. fresh **Mushrooms**
2 medium **Green Peppers**, sectioned
1/4 cup **Soy Sauce**
1/4 cup **Salad Oil**
1/4 cup **Lemon Juice**
1/4 cup chopped **Parsley**
Dash **Pepper**
1/2 tsp. **Salt**
12 slices **Bacon**

Thaw scallops (or shrimp) if frozen. Remove any shell particles and wash. Combine soy sauce, salad oil, juice, parsley, pepper and salt and pour over scallops. Let stand for 30 minutes, turning once.

Place mushrooms, pineapple and pepper pieces into a mixing bowl. Fry bacon slowly until cooked, but not crisp. Cut each slice of bacon in half.

Using long skewers, alternate scallops, pineapple, mushrooms, pepper pieces and bacon until skewers are filled. Place kabobs over mesquite coals and cook for six minutes. Turn and cook for additional four to six minutes. Serves 6.

Fish Kabobs

Courtesy Lucky Stores, Inc.

1 1/2 lbs. **Frozen Fish Fillets** (cut in 2-inch cubes)

Marinate the fish pieces in the following mixture for one hour before cooking:

2 cups **Garlic French Dressing**	1/2 tsp. crushed **Sweet Basil**
2 tbsp. **Lemon Juice**	1/2 tsp. crushed **Oregano**

Thread metal skewers with the following:

Bacon (cut in 4-inch pieces, folded in half)
Tomato Wedges
Green Onion (cut in 2-inch pieces)
Marinated Fish Fillets
Green Pepper Wedges

Allow 10 minutes cooking time, turning often, and continue to brush on marinade as kabobs cook.

Tip: To test the temperature of a fire— CAUTIOUSLY hold your hand, palm side down, at least four inches ABOVE the coals. Count off the seconds to test temperature:

2 seconds = it's HOT
3 seconds = it's Medium Hot
4 seconds = it's Medium
5 seconds = it's a Low Fire

Tip: Fish is done when it flakes against a fork.

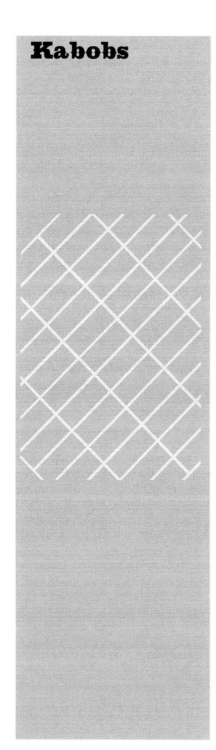

Fruit Kabobs with Whiskey Baste

Courtesy The Kingsford® Company

2 tbsp. **Honey**
2 tbsp. **Whiskey**
1 tbsp. **Lemon Juice**
1 can (8 oz.) **Pineapple Chunks**, drained
1 large **Banana**, bias sliced into 1-inch pieces
1 **Orange**, peeled and sectioned
8 **Maraschino Cherries**
4 **Skewers** (12-inch, bamboo or metal)

In a mixing bowl combine the honey, whiskey and lemon juice. Add pineapple chunks, banana pieces, orange sections and cherries. Gently toss to coat fruit well. Cover and refrigerate up to two hours until ready to grill.

Remove fruit with slotted spoon, reserving the whiskey baste to brush on fruit kabobs while grilling.

Alternately thread the fruit onto skewers. Grill the fruit kabobs on a covered grill, directly over moderately-low Kingsford® briquettes for five to ten minutes (or until fruit is warmed through). Makes four servings.

Note: If bamboo skewers are used, soak them in water for 20 minutes before using on the grill.

Pit Barbecue

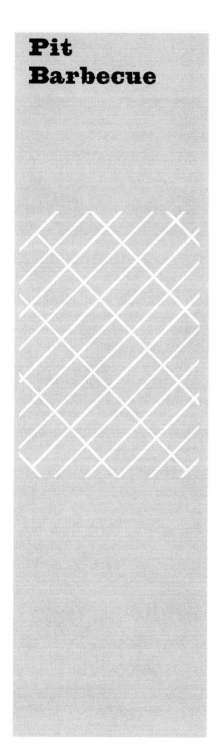

Pit Barbecue

Permanent Pit Barbecue

Sonny Martinez – Tucson, Arizona

Pit preparation:

Dig a pit that is about four feet wide, six feet long and three to four feet deep. Line the bottom and at least a foot up the sides with rocks.

Fill the pit with hardwood, such as mesquite or oak. Fill the pit with small pieces on the bottom and large chunks on the top. (The hardwood should provide a foot or two of good coals after burning for about two to four hours.)

Meat preparation:

Season the meat to taste. Coarse pepper, celery salt, chile pepper, garlic cloves and garlic powder are often used by barbecuers.

Wrap the meat in large quantities of old clean sheets, towels or cheesecloth, covering the meat with at least two layers. Just before putting the wrapped meat into the pit, wet down the coverings. Then, wet some burlap and wrap it around each meat package.

Drop the burlap-wrapped meat right onto the coals. Working rapidly, put metal pipe across the opening and cover with sheet metal. Cover the metal with several inches of clean dirt, MAKING SURE NO STEAM OR SMOKE IS ESCAPING.

Cook the meat for 10 to 12 hours. The meat can be checked at the end of cooking period and tested for doneness. Testing is done WITHOUT unwrapping the meat. If the wrapped meat feels soft—but not spongy—then it's done.

This size pit should easily cook 200 pounds of boneless meat.

Tip: Barbecue pits lined with bricks will keep dirt walls from caving in and will hold heat better.

Pit Barbecue

Larry Newham – Mesa, Arizona

Pit preparation:

Dig a trench three feet deep, 18 inches wide, and long enough to lay meat end to end. Start this two days in advance of barbecue. Lay hedge posts or mesquite posts in the trench. Ignite the posts and burn these until only hot coals are left. Coals should be at least 10 inches deep. The burning will take from six to eight hours. When coals are ready, cover with four inches of clean sand.

Meat preparation:

Allow one-half pound of meat per person. Use eight to ten pounds of beef brisket for each bundle of meat to be barbecued. Mix salt and pepper (average mix is one teaspoon of each) on all sides of meat. Wrap meat first in clean cheesecloth. Next, wrap each bundle of meat securely in a burlap sack.

Lay wrapped briskets end to end. Cover with tin, then layers of clean dirt, making an air-tight oven. Cook at least ten hours. Test to see if meat is done. (A new pitch-fork is ideal to put meat bundles into the trench.)

Tip: When a barbecue pit is properly sealed, the pit acts like a pressure cooker. If the pit is improperly sealed, the meat will burn.

Stump Farms Pit Barbecue

Bob Stump – Member of Congress (Arizona)

Pre-heat pit oven:

Dig a hole four feet wide, four feet deep and six feet long. Gather enough wood (preferably mesquite or other hardwood) to fill the hole. Light the fire approximately 24 hours prior to use. After the fire has burned for approximately 24 hours, you will have about two or three feet of hot coals.

Meat preparation:

Take ten chunks (10-lbs. each) of boneless chuck or any type of boneless meat. Season with Morton Sugar Cure® by rubbing liberally on meat. Shake off excess. If desired, sprinkle meat with garlic powder. Wrap each chunk in plain butcher paper and place in a WET burlap sack (available at feed stores). Tie each bundle tightly with wire. Have all sacks ready before placing any into the pit oven.

Barbecue:

Place all wet burlap-wrapped meat packages directly on top of coals. Cover with a piece of tin, leaving room for two to three feet of dirt which is to be placed on top of the tin. MAKE SURE THAT NO SMOKE ESCAPES. Smoke indicates ventilation and fire will occur. Bake for 24 hours. Dig up and serve. Serves 200.

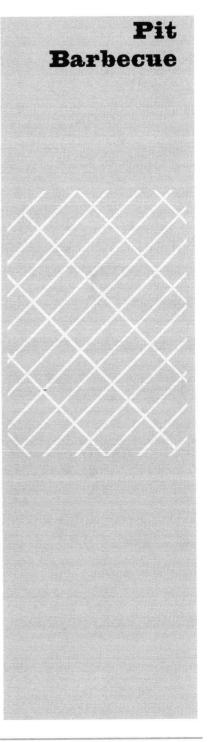

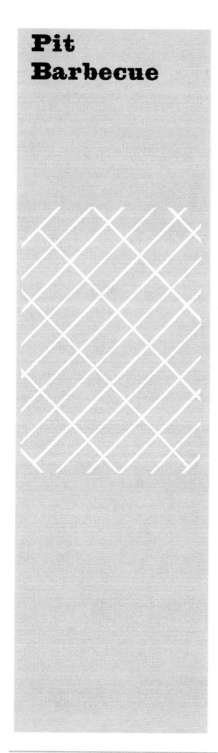

Chicken Roast

Larry Newham – Mesa, Arizona

Pit preparation:

Dig a pit three feet deep, 18 inches wide and long enough to hold the number of chickens needed. Use hedge posts or mesquite posts and burn until hot coals remain (about six to eight hours). Be sure to allow enough time for burning of logs. When bed of coals is ready, prepare chickens.

Chicken preparation:

Season 3-lb. chickens with salt and pepper, rubbing over entire chicken. Wrap each chicken first in a 30-inch square of clean cheesecloth. Next, wrap each in a layer of muslin. Dip each tightly-wrapped package in cold water. Using a pitchfork, lay packages on hot coals.

Partially cover packages with tin. Chickens will need to be turned with long-handled pitchfork to prevent burning. Cook for eight to ten hours, testing for doneness after eighth hour. (The tightly-wrapped chickens will stay wrapped if the turning is done carefully. Juices will keep the cloths wet and prevent burning.)

Fish and Seafood

Fish and Seafood

Tip: Use a medium-hot fire for fish. A too-hot fire will dry out a delicate fish.

Grilled Swordfish

Courtesy: The Kingsford® Company

4 fresh or frozen **Swordfish Steaks** (1/2-inch-thick—about 2 lbs.)

Thaw fish steaks, if frozen. Prepare marinade. Place fish in a shallow baking dish. Brush some of the cooled marinade over fish. Marinate fish for 30 minutes at room temperature.

Grill fish, on a covered grill, directly over medium-hot Kingsford® briquettes for four minutes. Brush with marinade. Turn and cook three to five minutes more (or until fish flakes easily when tested with a fork). Brush again with the marinade. Transfer to serving platter. Serves 4.

Marinade

1/3 cup **Tomato Paste** (half of a 6oz. can)
1/4 cup **Dry Red Wine**
6 cloves **Garlic**, sliced

1/8 tsp. ground **Red Pepper** (or few dashes of bottled **Hot Pepper Sauce**)
3 tbsp. snipped **Cilantro** or **Parsley**
2 tbsp. **Olive Oil**

In a small bowl, combine tomato paste, wine, garlic and red pepper. Put mixture into saucepan and bring to boiling. Reduce heat and simmer, covered, for one hour, stirring occasionally. Press through a sieve and discard garlic. Stir in cilantro and olive oil. Cool to room temperature.

Tip: A serving of fish is generally 1/3 to 1/2 pound of edible fish. For a whole fish, allow about one pound per person. For dressed fish, allow 1/2 pound per person.

Grilled Salmon

Hickory Specialties, Inc. – Brentwood, Tennessee

4 **Salmon Steaks** (one-inch thick)	2 large cloves **Garlic**
Oil (preferably **Olive Oil**)	1 tbsp. **Dried Dill**
Fresh **Ground Pepper** to taste	Juice of 1 **Lemon**

Wipe fish dry. Brush both sides with oil, then season on both sides with pepper. Crush the garlic cloves by hitting them with the back of a heavy spoon, and rub the salmon surfaces with the garlic. Sprinkle with dill and one-half the lemon juice.

Place over mesquite coals. Grill about 10-15 minutes. Sprinkle with the remaining lemon juice and serve immediately. Makes 4 servings.

Barbecued Red Snapper

Original recipes created by Master Chef Felipe Rojas Lombardi expressly for the Goya Foods, Inc. *Latin Barbecue a La Goya Cookbook*. All rights reserved.

4 1/2 lb. whole **Red Snapper** (with head and tail)	1 tbsp. **Goya® Adoba with Cumin**
	1 tsp. **Coarse Salt**
2 tbsp. **Goya® Recaito**	1/3 cup **Goya® Extra-Virgin**
2 tbsp. **Lemon Juice**	**Spanish Olive Oil**

Clean fish and cut fins off. Scale it again if necessary with a sharp scaling knife.

Prepare marinade by combining all ingredients in a bowl and mixing them thoroughly. Marinate fish for one to two hours in the refrigerator. If possible, wrap fish in banana leaves and then grill; the leaves give it an exotic taste. (Or use corn husks, aluminum foil, or a hinged fish grill). Serve with **Recaito Sauce a la Goya**.

Tip: To make turning easier, place fish in a flat, hinged wire basket especially made for the grill.

Recaito Sauce a la Goya

Original recipe created by Master Chef Felipe Rojas Lombardi expressly for the Goya Foods, Inc. *Latin Barbecue a la Goya Cookbook.* All rights reserved.

1/2 cup **Goya® Extra-Virgin Spanish Olive Oil**
2 large cloves **Garlic**, finely minced
1 cup finely chopped **Onion**
2 tbsp. finely chopped fresh **Ginger**
2 tbsp. **Goya® Hot Sauce**
4 tbsp. **Goya® Recaito**
1/4 cup **Water**
2 tbsp. **Lemon Juice**
1/4 tsp. **White Pepper**
1 tsp. **Sugar**
1/2 cup finely chopped **Coriander Leaves**
1/2 cup **La Vina White Cooking Wine**

Heat oil in saucepan, sauté garlic and ginger until golden. Add onions and sauté until translucent. Stir in other ingredients and simmer ten minutes. (This is salsa for fish. Makes two cups)

Note: Goya® Recaito is a puree of fresh green peppers, onions, garlic and fresh coriander, an authentic spice and condiment mixture distinctively Latin in taste.

Tip: Fish can be enhanced by buttering or flouring before it is placed on the grill. It should be brushed well with a marinade several times during cooking.

Barbecued Cod Fillets

2 lbs. **Cod Fillets**, fresh or frozen
2 tbsp. chopped **Onion**
1 clove **Garlic**, finely chopped
2 tbsp. **Oil**
1 can (8 oz.) **Tomato Sauce**

2 tbsp. **Sherry**
1/2 tsp. **Salt**
1/4 tsp. **Oregano**
3 drops **Liquid Hot Pepper Sauce**
Dash **Pepper**

Thaw frozen fillets. Cook onion and garlic in oil until tender. Add remaining ingredients and simmer for five minutes, stirring occasionally. Cool.

Cut fillets into serving-size portions and place in a single layer in a shallow baking dish. Pour sauce over fish and let stand for 30 minutes, turning once.

Remove fish, reserving sauce for basting. Place fish in well-greased, hinged wire grills. Cook about four inches from moderately hot coals for eight minutes. Baste with sauce. Turn and cook for seven to ten minutes longer or until fish flakes easily when tested with a fork. Serves 6.

Note: Halibut or similar fish steaks may be substituted for cod.

Striped Bass

2 lbs. **Striped Bass Steaks**
(fresh or frozen)
1/2 cup **Oil**
1/2 cup **Sesame Seeds**
1/3 cup **Cognac**

1/3 cup **Lemon Juice**
3 tbsp. **Soy Sauce**
1 tsp. **Salt**
1 large clove **Garlic**, crushed

Thaw frozen steaks. Cut into serving-size portions and place in a single layer in a shallow baking dish. Combine remaining ingredients. Pour sauce over fish and let stand for 30 minutes, turning once. Remove fish, reserving sauce for basting.

Place fish in well-greased, hinged wire grills. Cook about four inches from moderately hot coals for eight minutes. Baste with sauce. Turn and cook for seven to ten minutes longer or until fish flakes easily when tested with a fork. Serves 6.

Tip: To cook fresh fish on the grill, always oil grill rack with vegetable oil before placing fish on grill to prevent delicate skin from sticking.

Cantonese Shrimp Barbecue

Edna Chadsey – Corpus Christi, Texas

2 lbs. large **Shrimp** or 1 1/2 lbs. frozen, shelled **Shrimp**
3 thin slices preserved **Ginger**
2 tsp. **Ginger Syrup**
6 **Green Onions**, minced
1/4 cup **Dry White Wine**

3 tbsp. **Soy Sauce**
1/2 tsp. **Salt**
3 tbsp. **Sugar**
2 tbsp. **Vegetable Oil**
2 cloves **Garlic**, minced

Shell and devein shrimp, leaving tails intact. Mix remaining ingredients in large bowl. Marinate shrimp for two hours. Put shrimp on oiled skewers and grill three inches above hot charcoal about 4-5 minutes on each side. Brush several times with marinade and serve hot. Serves 6.

Grilled Striped Bass

2 lbs. **Striped Bass Steaks** (fresh or frozen)
1/2 cup **Oil**
1/2 cup **Sesame Seeds**
1/3 cup **Cognac**

1/3 cup **Lemon Juice**
3 tbsp. **Soy Sauce**
1 tsp. **Salt**
1 large clove **Garlic**, crushed

Thaw frozen steaks. Cut into serving-size portions and place in a single layer in a shallow baking dish. Combine remaining ingredients. Pour sauce over fish and let stand for 30 minutes, turning once. Remove fish, reserving sauce for basting.

Place fish in well-greased, hinged wire grills. Cook about four inches from moderately hot coals for eight minutes. Baste with sauce. Turn and cook for seven to ten minutes longer or until fish flakes easily when tested with a fork. Serves 6.

Citrus Swordfish

Barbecue Industry Association

1/2 cup **Orange Juice**
1/4 cup **Lemon Juice**
1 tbsp. **Olive Oil**
1 tsp. **Salt**
1 to 1 1/2-inch piece fresh **Ginger**, peeled and minced

1 large clove **Garlic**, peeled and minced
1/8 tsp. **Cayenne Pepper**
6 **Swordfish Steaks** (about 6 oz. each, cut 1-inch thick)

Prepare a hot charcoal fire. Combine juices, olive oil, salt, ginger, garlic and cayenne in a large non-aluminum pan and whisk until well blended.

Marinate swordfish at room temperature, turning several times.

Place fish on an oiled cooking grid set four to six inches above ashed coals. Grill, turning once and brushing with marinade, until fish is just opaque in the center, about 10 minutes. Serves 6.

Note: Halibut or tuna may be substituted for swordfish.

Chinese Barbecue Fish

Li-Chen Hillhouse – Live Oak, Florida

1 large **Fish** (4 to 8 lbs. Must be fresh, not frozen)
12 oz. **Tomato Paste**
1 medium **Onion**, chopped fine
1 clove **Garlic**
1/4 cup **Soy Sauce**

8 to 10 drops **Tabasco® Pepper Sauce**
2 tbsp. **Butter**
Dash **Black Pepper**
1/2 cup **Cooking Oil**

Clean fish and place whole fish in large bread pan. (Bass is good but salt water fish can also be used.) Combine remaining ingredients in small saucepan over low heat. DO NOT BOIL. Pour sauce over fish and put in 350 degree oven for 35 to 40 minutes (or until fish flakes when tested with fork). Serves 4 to 6.

Tip: For ease in barbecuing, put salmon steaks between the two portions of a long-handled, hinged basket accessory and set basket on cooking grid. Make sure basket is well oiled to prevent steaks from sticking.

Barbecued Alaskan Salmon Steaks

Barbecue Industry Association

4 **Alaskan Salmon Steaks** (6-8 oz. ea. fresh/frozen)
1/4 cup melted **Butter**
1 1/2 tsp. **Soy Sauce**
1 tbsp. **Lemon Juice**
1 tsp. **Worcestershire Sauce**
1 small clove **Garlic**, crushed
Dash **Tabasco® Pepper Sauce**
Liquid Smoke (few drops, optional)

Thaw steaks, if necessary. Combine remaining ingredients and mix well. Brush steaks generously with mixture. Place on oiled grill over hot coals. Grill, allowing 10 minutes per inch of thickness (or until salmon flakes easily with fork). Turn once halfway through cooking time. Baste frequently with marinade during cooking and once after taking salmon off grill. Serves 4.

Fish and Seafood

Recipe:_____

From:_____

Ingredients:

_____   _____

_____   _____

_____   _____

_____   _____

Directions:_____

_____

_____

_____

_____

Recipe:_____

From:_____

Ingredients:

_____   _____

_____   _____

_____   _____

_____   _____

Directions:_____

_____

_____

_____

_____

Side Dishes

Side Dishes

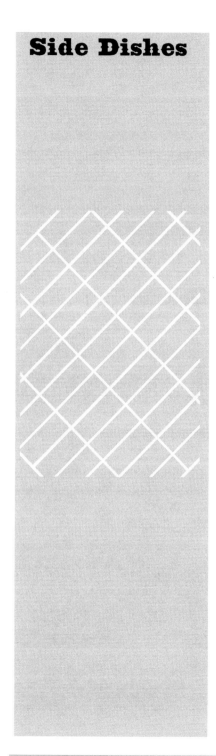

Potato Salad

3 lbs. **Potatoes**
2 cups diced **Celery**
1/4 cup finely chopped **Onion**
1/4 cup finely chopped **Parsley**
1 cup **Mayonnaise**

2 tsp. **Vinegar**
1 tsp. **Salt**
1/4 tsp. ground **Black Pepper**
Tomatoes (for garnish)

Cook potatoes in boiling water until tender. Peel and chill. Thinly slice chilled potatoes into mixing bowl. Add celery, onion, parsley, mayonnaise, vinegar, salt and pepper. Toss lightly until well mixed. Garnish with tomato slices. Serves 8.

Chunky Potato Salad

4 **Potatoes**
1/2 cup chopped **Celery**
1/3 cup chopped **Onion**
3/4 cup **Mayonnaise**

1/4 cup **Milk**
1 tsp. **Salt**
1/4 tsp. ground **Black Pepper**
1 tbsp. chopped **Parsley** (optional)

Peel potatoes and cut into halves. Put halves into pan and add an inch of water. Bring water to a boil, cover potatoes, lower heat and simmer 20 minutes (until tender). Drain off cooking liquid when potatoes are done.

While potatoes are simmering, combine remaining ingredients into a salad bowl. Cut warm potatoes into chunks and add to salad bowl. Chill thoroughly before serving. Makes 4 to 6 servings.

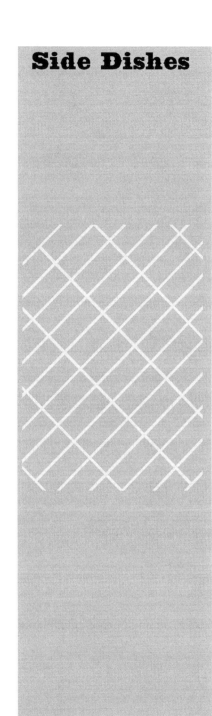

Hot Potato Salad

1/2 tsp. **Powdered Mustard**
1/2 tsp. **Water**
1 tbsp. **Butter** or **Margarine**
1 tbsp. **Flour**
1/2 tsp. **Salt**
1 tsp. **Sugar**
1/8 tsp. **Black Pepper**
1/2 cup **Water**

1/2 cup **Tarragon Vinegar**
1 large **Egg Yolk**, beaten
6 cups hot sliced **Potatoes**
2 tbsp. finely chopped **Onion**
2 large **Eggs**, hard-boiled, diced
1 cup diced **Celery**
Sliced stuffed **Olives**

Combine mustard and water and set aside for 10 minutes. Melt butter and stir in flour, salt, sugar and pepper until smooth. Gradually add water and vinegar, stirring until smooth.

Pour a little of the hot mixture into the beaten egg. Stir to mix well. Add to vinegar and cook one minute. Remove from heat. Combine next three ingredients and stir to mix well.

Pour hot sauce over the potato mixture and toss lightly. Add celery. Serve hot topped with olive slices. Serves 8.

Eastern-Style Slaw

North Carolina Pork Producers Association

6 medium heads (about 36 cups)
   Cabbage, finely shredded
1 1/2 cups sliced **Green Onion**
1 1/2 quarts **Mayonnaise**
   (or salad dressing)

3/4 cup **Sugar**
3/4 cup **Vinegar**
2 to 4 tbsp. **Celery Seed**
2 tbsp. **Salt** (or to taste)

Combine cabbage and onion in a large bowl. In a smaller bowl, blend mayonnaise, sugar, vinegar, celery seed and salt. Mix well and drizzle mayonnaise mixture over cabbage mix. Toss lightly to coat well. Refrigerate until serving. Serves 50.

Marcia's Sweet-Sour Slaw

Marcia Cernoch – Rosenberg, Texas

1 medium **Cabbage**, finely grated or chopped
1 medium **Onion**, sliced in fine circles
2 **Carrots**, peeled and sliced in thin circles
2 **Green Peppers**, sliced in thin circles
Salt and **Pepper** to taste
1 cup **Vinegar**
1 cup **Sugar**
1 cup **Salad Oil**

Be sure that the onions, carrots and peppers are sliced very thin. Mix the vegetables, season with salt and pepper. Then add vinegar, sugar and salad oil to vegetables, mixing thoroughly. Serves 10.

Home-Style Cole Slaw

2 tbsp. **Vinegar**
1 cup **Mayonnaise**
1 tsp. **Salt**
1/2 tsp. **Sugar**
1/2 tsp. **Black Pepper**
1/2 tsp. grated **Onion**
1 medium head **Cabbage** (about 10 cups shredded)
2 **Carrots**, shredded
1/4 **Green Pepper**, shredded

Combine vinegar with mayonnaise and stir until well blended. Add salt, sugar, pepper and onion and mix thoroughly. Chill until serving. Combine shredded cabbage, carrots and green pepper and toss with mayonnaise mixture until thoroughly coated. Makes 8 servings.

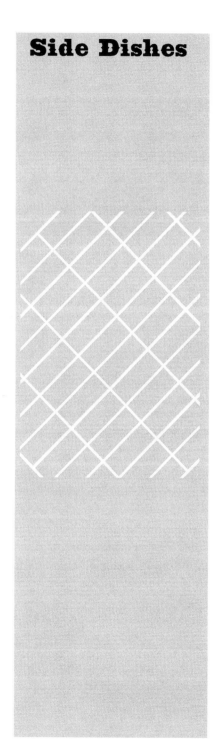

Arizona Dutch Oven Yeast Rolls

Dilworth Brinton – Mesa, Arizona

4 pkgs. **Yeast** dissolved in 4 1/2 cups **Lukewarm Water**
4 **Eggs**
6 tbsp. **Sugar** (one of which is mixed into yeast)
2 tbsp. **Salt**
1 cup **Powdered Milk**
1 cup **Wesson® Oil**
4 lbs. **Flour** (approximate)
5 to 8 pie or cake pans (to fit Dutch oven)

Combine all ingredients and mix thoroughly. Dough should be soft and sticky. Let stand about 20 to 30 minutes. Roll dough out from one-half-to three-fourths-inch thick. Cut with roll cutter (a Vienna sausage can is ideal—punch a hole in the top so roll will drop out). Dip cut rolls lightly into oil in a quick, flip-flop motion to keep rolls from sticking to the pan. Shape dough into Parkerhouse-style rolls (folded over). Put rolls into pie pan or cake pans and let rise.

Cook in Dutch oven with coals top and bottom. Put three small rocks (or bottle caps) in bottom of oven and put cooking pan on these to prevent burning on the bottom. Makes approximately 100 rolls.

Note: If you bake in large quantities, get one-pound blocks of yeast from a store or bakery (32 cakes per one-pound package).

Self-Frosting Cinnamon Rolls

Prepare recipe as on the previous page, EXCEPT add six 6 tablespoons more sugar. If desired, a half-pound of raisins may be added to the dough during mixing. Roll dough one-half-inch thick (or less) and about six to eight inches wide. Sprinkle dough with brown sugar and cinnamon, and roll into jelly roll shape for cutting. (Pinch edges to hold.)

Cut sections one-inch thick and place in prepared pan, leaving room for expansion. Brush on top with melted oleo.

To Prepare Pans

Pour three tablespoons melted oleo into baking pan. Sprinkle in brown sugar to cover bottom. Add chopped nuts. Put rolls into pan on top of sugar and nuts. Let rise and bake. Turn out of pan immediately when done. Makes approximately 100 self-frosted cinnamon rolls.

Dutch-Oven Biscuits

Denvon Rogers – Mesa, Arizona

4 cups **Self-Rising Flour**	1 1/2 cups **Milk**
2 tsp. **Baking Powder**	1/4 cup **Oil**
3 tsp. **Sugar**	

Blend together the flour, baking powder and sugar. Then add milk and mix. Stir in oil. Pour out on a floured board and pat out until about one-half-inch thick. Cut into biscuits.

Bake in a hot Dutch-oven with a few hot coals under the oven and hot coals completely covering the lid. Bake until golden brown (about 20 minutes). Makes about 14 biscuits.

Hush Puppies

North Carolina Pork Producers Association

3 1/2 cups **Water**
2 cups **Corn Meal**
1 tsp. **Baking Powder**
1 tbsp. **Sugar**

1 tsp. **Salt**
1 medium **Onion**, finely chopped
1/4 cup softened **Butter**

Bring water to a boil. Combine cornmeal, baking powder, sugar, salt and onion. Add slowly to boiling water, stirring constantly until mixture is smooth. Remove from heat. Add butter, stirring until melted. Cool mixture ten minutes.

Shape batter into 2 × 1 inch oblong rolls. Deep fry in hot oil (375 degrees), cooking only a few at a time. Fry until hush puppies are golden brown. Drain well on paper towels. Serve hot. Makes 3 1/2 dozen.

Hush Puppies

North Carolina Pork Producers Association

5 lbs. self-rising **Corn Meal**
1/2 cup self-rising **Flour**
2 tbsp. **Sugar**
2 1/2 quarts (or more) **Water**
    and **Buttermilk**
    (or 2 1/2 quarts of either)

1/2 cup melted **Shortening**
    (optional)
3 tbsp. minced **Onion**
    (optional)
4 **Eggs** (optional)

Stir liquid into dry ingredients, making a thick batter. (The addition of shortening improves texture. Onion adds flavor. Eggs improve texture and flavor.) Drop from spoon into fat which has been heated to 350-375 degrees. Fry to a golden brown. Makes 125 to 150.

Tip: Palm Oil can be used as a substitute for partially hydrogenated fats.

Cowboy's Border Beans

Courtesy Susan Nunn – Tempe, Arizona

Water to fill a tall pot half-full
2 1/2 lbs. **Dry Pinto Beans**
1/2 lb. **Ham Hock** or **Salt Pork**
6 cloves **Garlic**, finely chopped

2 tsp. **Dried Oregano**
10 **Chili Pequenos**, mashed
2 tsp. **Lemon Juice** or **Salt**

Add beans to pot (half-filled with water) and bring to a boil over medium heat. Stir frequently to prevent burning. Reduce heat to slow simmer and cook five hours uncovered, letting beans "pack." Do not stir, but add boiling water to keep beans covered.

Then, in sequence, add the following, but DO NOT STIR:

after 1st hour, add ham hock (or salt pork).
after 2nd hour, add garlic.
after 3rd hour, add oregano and chilies.
after 4th hour, add lemon juice (or salt).
after 5th hour, serve beans.
Makes four quarts.

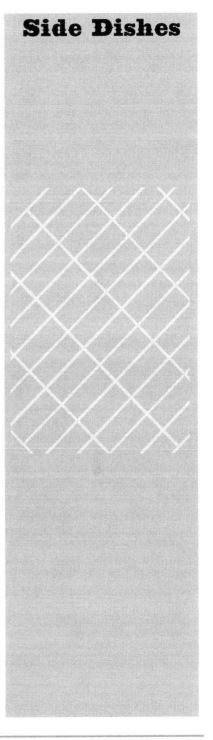

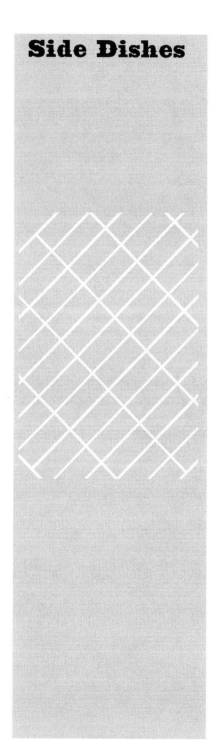

Cowboy Beans

Sharon Pinnell – Helotes TX

2 lb. **Dry Pinto Beans**
1 tbsp. **Granulated Onion**
1 tbsp. **Red Chile Powder**
1 tsp. **Granulated Garlic**
1 tsp. **Chicken Bouillon Crystals**
1 large <u>cured</u> **Ham Hock**

½ tsp. **Cumin**
¼ tsp. **Black Pepper**
1 tsp. **Brown Sugar**
1 tsp. **Salt**
2-3 **Jalapeño Peppers**, diced
Bits of **Smithfield Ham** (optional)

Wash beans, soak overnight, rinse. Pour into a pot with 12 cups of water. Bring to a boil. Cook for 1 hour. Add ham hock and remaining ingredients. Cook covered for 2 hours or until done. Add water as needed. To cook, hang Dutch oven with handle on a tripod with a hot bed of coals under the pot. Check often for water, depending on where you are cooking, water can evaporate fast. If you do not have a tripod for cooking; set Dutch oven over hot coals and add hot coals to the lid.

Note: For Borracho Beans add 2 bottles of dark beer…like a stout.
        In place of granulated onion; use 1 small onion, chopped.
        In place of water, use vegetable broth

Barbecue Beans

Roger Wagner – Phoenix, Arizona

7 cups **Barbecue Sauce**
6 cans (10 oz. Each) **Pinto Beans**, drained
2 cups chopped **Onions**
2 cups chopped **Green Pepper**

2 oz. each of cooked **Beef**, **Pork** and **Ham**
1 cup **Molasses**
1 tbsp. **Chili Powder**
1 tbsp. **Salt**
1 tbsp. **Black Pepper**

Combine all ingredients. Bake at 350 degrees for 1 1/2 hours. Makes 25 servings.

Western Beans

Dian Broening – Mesa, Arizona

1/2 lb. **Dry Pinto Beans**	1/4 cup firmly packed **Dark Brown Sugar**
1/2 lb. **Pork Fat** (or bacon cut into one-inch squares)	1 1/2 tsp. **Salt**
1 clove **Garlic**, minced or pressed	1/2 tsp. **Chili Powder**
1 cup chopped **Onion**	Dash **Cayenne Pepper**
1 cup **Tomato Juice**	1 **Apple**, peeled and thinly sliced

Soak beans overnight in cold water. Next day, drain and put beans into a three-quart saucepan. Cover with boiling water and heat to boiling. Reduce heat, cover and simmer for two hours.

Fry pork fat (or bacon) in large skillet, breaking up with spoon as it cooks. Add garlic and onion. Then add tomato juice, brown sugar, salt, chili powder and cayenne to bacon. Reduce heat, cover and simmer for 30 minutes.

Add bacon mixture and apple to beans. Heat to boiling. Reduce heat, cover and simmer for 30 minutes. Serves 6.

Barbequed Beans

Larry Newham – Mesa, Arizona

2 lbs. **Pinto Beans**	1/4 cup **Brown Sugar**
1 tsp. **Salt**	6 slices **Bacon**, cut up
1 tsp. **Chili Powder**	1 cup **Barbecue Sauce**

Wash beans and add to a two-quart crock pot. Cover with water and cook on high. When beans have boiled 30 minutes, drain and rinse. Return to crock pot. Add remaining ingredients and water to cover. (More water should be added as needed for beans to be covered.) Cook on high six to eight hours OR on low for ten to twelve hours. Can be served immediately or cooled down and refrigerated.

Tip: Line the grill with heavy-duty aluminum foil for fast cooking and even faster clean-up.

Simple and Great Foiled Potatoes

Steven R. Sutter – Bluffton, Ohio

2 small **Potatoes**
1 **Onion**, cut into thin pieces
3 tbsp. **Butter**

1 tsp. **Salt**
1/2 tsp. **Black Pepper**
1/2 clove **Garlic**, cut into small pieces

Put all ingredients into an aluminum foil packet and seal ends tightly. Put a second foil packet over the first one and seal securely. Cook over hot to medium coals about 45 minutes to one hour, turning often (taking care not to puncture packets).

Mashed Potatoes

Chuck wagon cookin'

Sharon Pinnell – Helotes TX

4 cups **Mashed Potatoes**, about 2 lbs. diced potatoes
Milk or **Sour Cream** to blend potatoes
¼ cup diced **Lean Bacon** (buy center cut)
1 medium **Onion**, cut in ½ and thinly sliced
½ cup shredded **Cheddar** or **Parmesan Cheese**
2 cloves **Garlic**, minced (cook with bacon and onion)

Prepare mashed potatoes as usual, omitting butter. (Make sure you keep enough water over the potatoes when cooking with hot coals). In a heavy skillet over fire fry bacon and onion together with garlic. Add to potatoes, mixing thoroughly. Check for seasoning. Top with cheese when ready to serve. Season with salt and pepper. These potatoes taste like a baked potato. Double or triple for Chuck wagon Dutch oven competition.

✎Tip: To keep vegetables moist, brush them with oil before grilling.

Barbecued Corn-on-the Cob

Strip husks down to end of cob, but do not remove. Tear off silk threads. Allow husked corn to stand in cold, salted water for ten minutes. Brush corn with softened **Butter** or **Margarine** and season with **Salt** and **Pepper**. Bring husks back up around cob (making sure entire ear is covered). Secure husks with picture-hanging wire or strip of cornhusk tied tightly.

Place ears in double thickness of heavy-duty aluminum foil (twisting foil ends securely). Place on briquettes for about ten minutes (turning once).

When corn is done, remove wire and husks, and serve immediately.

Seasoned Butters for Corn-on-the-Cob

Combine one-half cup (one stick) **Butter** (softened) with **one** of the following:

- 1/2 teaspoon **Curry Powder** or **Chili Powder**
- 1/2 teaspoon **Hickory Smoked Salt**
- 1 teaspoon **Chopped Chives** or **Parsley**
- 1 teaspoon **Herb Seasoning** (finely ground).

Makes enough seasoned butter for six to eight ears of corn.

Tip: Stack briquettes in a pyramid. They will light faster since air can circulate.

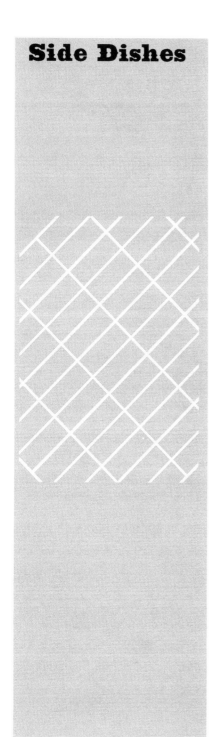

Grilled Vegetables

By Permission: Lea & Perrins, Inc.

1 cup **Carrots** (cut in strips)*
1 cup **Zucchini** (cut in strips)*
1 cup **Onion Wedges**
1 cup **Green Peppers** (cut in 1/2-inch strips)
2 tbsp. **Lea & Perrins® Steak Sauce**
2 tbsp. **Water**
4 tbsp. **Butter** or **Margarine**

Combine all vegetables, Lea & Perrins® Steak Sauce and water. Mix well. For each portion, place one cup of the vegetable mixture into the center of a 12-inch square of aluminum foil. Top with one teaspoon butter. Bring edges of foil together and seal securely. Repeat for each portion.

To cook over charcoal, place packets on a rack over slow-burning coals until vegetables are crisp-tender (about 30-minutes) turning packets often. Makes 4 portions.

*Strips: 2 inches long × 1/4-inch thick

Vegetable Bundles

Place any of the following vegetables on heavy-duty foil (12-inch squares). Season and dot with **Butter**. Use a double fold at top and ends to secure bundle. Grill over medium heat as indicated:

Medium, whole **Mushrooms**: 10 to 12 minutes
Carrots and **Zucchini** (sliced diagonally): 25 minutes
Unpeeled Potatoes (sliced): 30 minutes
Green Pepper Strips: 30 minutes.

Allow enough vegetables to serve four.

Foil-Baked Apples

4 medium **Cooking Apples**, cored   Raisins
1/2 cup **Brown Sugar**   Water
2 tsp. **Butter** or **Margarine**

Cut about one inch of peel from top of each apple. Stand each apple in a piece of heavy-duty foil (or double layer of regular strength foil) large enough to cover individual apple completely.

Fill each apple core with following:

1 to 2 tbsp. **Brown Sugar**   Sprinkling of **Raisins**
1/2 tsp. **Butter**

Bring corners of foil together on apples and spoon 1 1/2 teaspoons of water into each foil packet. With apples standing right side up, seal edges of foil securely. Place foil-wrapped apples around edge of coals. Rotate apples two or three times during cooking period, taking care to have apples standing right side up. Apples will take about 45 to 55 minutes to bake.

Test by carefully unwrapping foil and piercing apples with a fork. Apples should be fork tender. When done, remove from foil and serve in bowl with syrup remaining in packet. Add heavy cream, if desired. Serves 4.

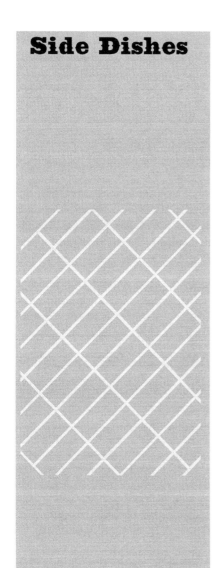

Bananas Foster

Courtesy The Reynolds Wrap® Kitchens

3 medium **Bananas**
1/4 cup **Butter** or **Margarine**
1/4 cup firmly packed **Brown Sugar**

2 tsp. **Rum Extract**
1/4 tsp. **Cinnamon**
Vanilla Ice Cream

Tear off a length of Heavy Duty Reynolds Wrap®. Slice bananas in half lengthwise and crosswise. Place bananas in center of foil sheet. Dot with butter. Sprinkle with brown sugar, rum extract and cinnamon.

Bundle wrap bananas by bringing four corners of foil up together in a pyramid shape. Fold the openings together loosely to allow for heat circulation and expansion. Seal by folding over ends and pressing to the package. Grill over medium hot coals 15 to 20 minutes, or until bananas are tender.

To serve, spoon into serving dishes and top with ice cream. Serves 4.

Granny Gillis' Pickled Peaches

Othalyne Gillis – Douglas, Georgia

2 cans (29 oz. each) **Peach Halves**
1 1/3 cups **Sugar**
1 cup **Apple Cider Vinegar**

5 **Cinnamon Sticks**
2 tbsp. **Whole Cloves**

Drain juice from peaches and save. Mix juice, sugar and vinegar. Tie whole cloves in cheesecloth, then add cinnamon sticks and cloves to juice mixture. Bring to a boil and simmer five minutes.

After mixture has cooled (it's ok to refrigerate it), add peaches and store in refrigerator. Will keep up to two months. Recipe may be doubled.

Paprika Potatoes

Courtesy Barbecue Industry Association

Red New Potatoes
Olive Oil

Salt and Pepper
Paprika

Boil (or microwave) tiny red new potatoes until just tender. When cool enough to handle, slice in half and thread on skewers. Brush lightly with olive oil and season well with salt, pepper and paprika. Grill, turning several times, until potatoes are crispy brown on the outside and fork-tender inside (about 10 minutes).

Quick and Cheesy Tomatoes

Courtesy Barbecue Industry Association

Tomatoes
Olive Oil

Salt and Pepper
Grated Cheese

Brush thick slices of ripe red tomatoes with olive oil and season with salt and pepper. Grill until lightly browned (about two to three minutes). Turn carefully with a wide metal spatula. Top each tomato slice with some grated cheese and grill until cheese just begins to soften and tomatoes are tender, but still hold their shape (about two minutes longer).

Smoky Onions

Courtesy Barbecue Industry Association

3 large Red Onions
Olive Oil

Salt and Pepper

Cut three large red onions into half-inch-thick slices. Brush with olive oil and season with salt and pepper. Grill, turning once or twice with a wide metal spatula, until onions are lightly browned and tender (about six to ten minutes).

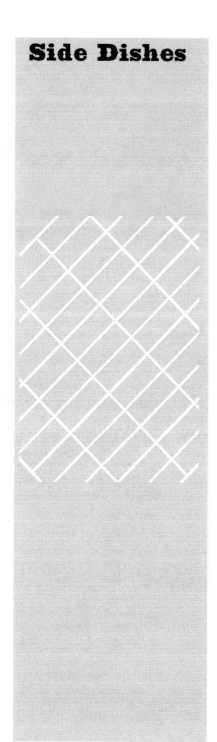

Lemony Green Beans

Courtesy Barbecue Industry Association

Green Beans, trimmed
Olive Oil
Salt and **Pepper**

Scallions, chopped
Lemon, thinly sliced

Make six packets from a double-thickness of aluminum foil and fill with individual portions of trimmed young, tender green beans tossed with olive oil. Season with salt, pepper and chopped scallions. Before crimping each packet closed, top with a thin slice of lemon. Place packets, seam-side up, around the cooler edges of the cooking grid. Cook until beans are just crisp-tender (about 12 to 15 minutes).

Hurricane Pineapple

Courtesy Barbecue Industry Association

Fresh **Pineapple**
4 tbsp. melted **Butter**

1 tbsp. **Rum**

Cut a fresh pineapple into half-inch-thick slices (or use well-drained canned pineapple rings. Melt four tablespoons of sweet butter with a tablespoon of rum in a small pot placed on the side of the cooking grid. Grill pineapple, turning occasionally and brushing with rum butter, until lightly browned yet still slightly firm (about 10 to 12 minutes).

Meet the Author

Cooking and exchanging recipes occupy a prominent place in this author's life. In preparation for her fourth book collection of recipes, Mildred Fischer examined hundreds of barbecue ideas which were submitted to her publisher in a national contest. In addition, she was in touch with a variety of barbecue associations throughout the country in order to create a contemporary barbecue book.

Her earlier cook books (written in conjunction with her husband) are *Arizona Cook Book*, *Chili-Lovers' Cook Book*, *California Country Cook Book* and *Citrus Lovers Cook Book*.

In addition to an enthusiasm for culinary delights, Mildred is an ardent theatre-goer, world traveler and museum buff. Her interest in theatre led her to write *London Theatre Today* (a guidebook to the theatres in London). Following a motor-home sojourn in Mexico, she wrote *Mexico's West Coast Beaches*.

Since Arizona has been her home for many years, she visited all the museums in that state to write a photo-guide, *Arizona Museums*.

Her world travels have taken her to Hawaii, China, the Soviet Union, England, Greece, Italy, Sicily, Canada, Mexico, and parts of northern and central Europe.

Professionally, Mrs. Fischer teaches a variety of English subjects—including mythology and creative writing— at Glendale Community College.

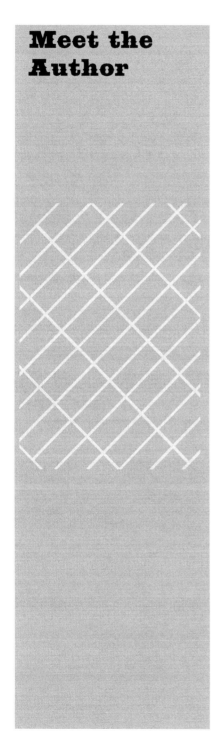

Meet the Author

She lives with her husband Al in Phoenix, Arizona; they are parents of three grown children.

Always interested in ways to prepare foods, Mildred Fischer has gathered a host of unusual and tried-and-true recipes for her *Best Barbecue Recipes*.

Salsa Lovers Cookbook
More than 180 recipes for
salsa, dips, salads, appetizers
and more!
$9.95

Quick-n-Easy Mexican Recipes
Make your favorite Mexican
dishes in record time! Excellent
tacos, tostadas, enchiladas
and more!
$9.95

Chip and Dip Lovers Cookbook
Easy and colorful recipes from
Southwestern salsas to quick
appetizer dips!
$9.95

Tortilla Lovers' Cookbook
Celebrate the tortilla with more than
100 easy recipes for breakfast, lunch,
dinner, appetizers and desserts, too!
$9.95

Chili Lovers Cookbook
Prize-winning recipes for chili,
with or without beans. Plus a
variety of taste-tempting foods
made with flavorful chile peppers.
$9.95

Arizona Cookbook
A collection of more than 350
authentic Arizona recipes.
Including Indian, Mexican. and
Western foods.
$9.95

New Mexico Cookbook
This unique book explores the
age-old recipes that are rich with
the heritage of New Mexico.
$9.95

Easy RV Recipes
Easy recipes for the traveling cook.
Over 200 recipes to make in your
RV, camper or houseboat.
$9.95

Easy Recipes for Wild Game
More than 200 "wild" recipes
for large and small game,
wild fowl and fish.
$9.95

Apple Lovers Cookbook
What's more American than eating
apple pie? Try these 150 favorite
recipes for appetizers, main and
side dishes, muffins, pies, salads,
beverages and preserves.
$9.95

Pumpkin Lovers Cookbook
More than 175 recipes for soups,
breads, muffins, pies, cakes, cheese-
cakes, cookies and even ice cream!
Carving tips, trivia and more.
$9.95

Mexican Family Favorites Recipes
250 authentic, homestyle recipes for
tacos, tamales, menudo, enchiladas,
burros, salsas, frijoles, carne seca, chile
rellenos, guacamole, and more!
$9.95

ORDER BLANK

GOLDEN WEST COOKBOOKS

☼ **5738 North Central Avenue • Phoenix, AZ 85012**

www.GoldenWestCookbooks.com • 1-800-521-9221 • FAX 602-234-3062

Qty	Title	Price	Amount
	Apple Lovers Cookbook	9.95	
	Arizona Cookbook	9.95	
	Bean Lovers Cookbook	9.95	
	Best Barbecue Recipes	14.95	
	Chili-Lovers' Cookbook	9.95	
	Chip and Dip Lovers Cookbook	9.95	
	Cowboy Cookbook	9.95	
	Easy Recipes for Wild Game	9.95	
	Easy RV Recipes	9.95	
	Grand Canyon Cookbook	9.95	
	Low Fat Mexican Recipes	9.95	
	New Mexico Cookbook	9.95	
	Mexican Family Favorites Cookbook	9.95	
	Peach Lovers Cookbook	9.95	
	Pecan Lovers Cookbook	9.95	
	Quick-n-Easy Mexican Recipes	9.95	
	Salsa Lovers Cookbook	9.95	
	Seafood Lovers Cookbook	9.95	
	Sedona Cookbook	9.95	
	Tequila Cookbook	9.95	
	Texas Cookbook	9.95	
	Tortilla Lovers Cookbook	9.95	
	Veggie Lovers Cookbook	9.95	
	Western Breakfast	9.95	
U.S. Shipping & Handling Add:		1-3 Books $3.00	
(Shipping to all other countries see website.)		4+ Books $5.00	
		Arizona residents add 9.3% sales tax	

Total $_____
(Payable in U.S. funds)

☐ My Check or Money Order Enclosed
☐ MasterCard ☐ VISA ☐ Discover ☐ American Express Verification code_____

Acct. No._____ Exp. Date_____

Signature_____

Name_____ Phone_____

Address_____ Email_____

City/State/Zip_____

Call for a FREE catalog of all our titles — Prices subject to change —